When Faith Turns Ugly

When Faith Turns Ugly

Understanding Toxic Faith and How to Avoid It

Brian Harris

First published 2016 by Paternoster
Paternoster is an imprint of Authentic Media Ltd,
PO Box 6326, Bletchley, Milton Keynes MK1 9GG
authenticmedia.co.uk

British Library Cataloguing in Publication Data

A catalogue record for this book is available from the British Library

ISBN 978-1-84227-857-4
978-1-78078-341-3 (e-book)

Cover design by David McNeill revocreative.co.uk

Dedicated to my children and their spouses:
Nic and Cat,
Amy and Aaron,
Jett.
They are a perpetual source of joy, hope and inspiration.
Their Christian faith is deep and transforming. They plan
to pass it on to the next generation . . .

Contents

Preface

It was an unexpected encounter at an art gallery and it left me unsettled and concerned. Rosemary and I had been admiring the entries for the Mandorla Art Award and were impressed by the wide array of interpretations given to its 2014 theme, 'Elijah Meets God'. One of the viewers did not share our enthusiasm, and started to mutter angrily to me, 'How can they allow an exhibition like this? Don't they know anything about the Bible? It's such a bloodthirsty book. And how can they have a competition about Elijah? He killed off all his religious opponents. Religion, that's the problem with the world today; and now they're trying to sanitize it with this art award.'

I tried to present an alternative point of view, but he would have none of it. He appeared to be an ethically sensitive person, but at the deepest level of his being he seemed to find the idea of religion offensive. I wondered if he might feel a little differently about Jesus, as many people separate their views of institutionalized faith from their feelings about Christ, but he turned out to be as vigorous an opponent of Jesus as he was of Elijah. 'Clearly you have never really examined his claims,' he told me. 'Fancy announcing that you are the only way, truth and life and that no one can get to God except through you. It's the breeding ground of intolerance, and look at the harvest of religious wars it has reaped.'

Again, my attempts to defend Jesus got nowhere. He left the gallery shortly afterwards, clearly annoyed that he had stumbled into a display that so offended his ethical sensibilities.

I have been a follower of Jesus for over forty years. During that time I have often encountered people who have expressed intellectual reservations about the trustworthiness of the Christian faith. As both a student and a teacher of apologetics, I have grappled with their questions and have, at least to my own satisfaction, resolved the majority of them. The remainder I have learnt to live with. They don't seem too significant to me. More recently, however, I have noticed a different tone to the objections. People seem a little less interested in debating whether miracles can or cannot happen, or if the Bible can or cannot be trusted. Their issue is no longer primarily with the question of truth, but with the question of moral credibility.

It has taken me by surprise, and I have spent the last few years wrestling with some of the issues raised. To me it has always seemed a self-evident truth that Christianity is a force for good in the world. I have seen so many faith-based projects bring light and hope to otherwise bleak and depressing landscapes. And I have met so many wonderful people whose faith in Jesus has touched and shaped them in such a way that their kindness and goodness spontaneously overflow into the lives of all who come into contact with them. I struggle to understand why people would question their integrity and morality – or the worthiness of the faith that has led to this transformation.

Perhaps it has been the many financial scandals in which the church has become embroiled. And then there are the heartbreaking cases of sexual abuse by the clergy – so many of them . . . And then there are the many examples of the abuse of power by religious leaders. If money, sex and power are the three false gods of our age, the church at times has been guilty of bowing down to each. The consequences are increasingly apparent. A watching world no longer believes that Christian leaders can be trusted, or that they have anything to contribute to the resolution of the ethical issues of our age. Faith is increasingly marginalized to a purely private zone, its presence in the public arena distrusted, unwelcome and often forbidden. How has it come to this?

We need to acknowledge that while faith (and in this book I usually limit myself to the Christian faith) can be life-serving, it can also turn toxic. As with Jekyll and Hyde, you cannot always be sure just which version you will get . . . or can you?

I have become increasingly convinced that it is possible to differentiate between forms of faith that are likely to do good in the world, and those that do damage – sometimes deeply destructive damage. But it is not only possible to differentiate between different kinds of faith, it is also imperative that we do so. We need to spot the signs that faith is at risk of turning venomous. We must move beyond the naive silliness that assumes that simply because something has a religious veneer it must be supported and defended. Not all forms of faith do good; some do great damage, and it is important that we acknowledge this openly and transparently. Indeed, we have a responsibility to warn people against embracing toxic faith, and we should alert them to some of the signs that faith is in danger of becoming destructive.

That is why I have written this book.

Many of my friends will find it a surprising read. They know me to be an instinctive optimist, able to spot the hopeful in even the gloomiest scenarios. They will wonder why I have highlighted the negative. Actually, I hope I have not. While I have become increasingly aware that faith can turn us into people who listen poorly and who arrogantly assume we already have the answer to every question, I am more than ever convinced that genuine Christ-following leads us in a different direction. And I long that all those who desire to serve and follow God will be spared the destructive paths that might lead them astray.

This book is the third I have written for Paternoster. I am deeply grateful to them and to their commissioning editor, Dr Michael Parsons, for the support and encouragement provided. They have allowed me to write on three of my great interests.

My first book, *The Tortoise Usually Wins: Biblical Reflections on Quiet Leadership for Reluctant Leaders* (Paternoster, 2013), explores the area of quiet leadership. In its own way it is not unrelated to the issues raised in this book, for often a cause of toxic faith is the embrace of unhelpful and sub-biblical models of leadership. This book tries to provide a hopeful alternative.

My second Paternoster book, *The Big Picture: Building Blocks of a Christian World View* (Paternoster, 2015), examines the contours of the Christian faith and investigates the key building blocks of what we believe. It tries to get to the heart of what really matters in each of these beliefs. Again, the material is not unrelated to the topic of this book, as faulty beliefs bolster defective expressions of faith.

And so we now come to the third and final of this mini-series: *When Faith Turns Ugly: Toxic Faith and How to Avoid It.* I am so grateful to those who have made this project possible.

Vose Seminary, the theological college where I have the privilege of serving as principal, has been an ideal setting for my writing. Its students and staff raise the right questions. They are committed to genuinely following Jesus the Christ. They have no interest in being sidetracked by subcultural expressions of faith. They realize that far too much is at stake.

Carey Community Baptist Church, where I serve as 'pastor at large', is another ideal context. Committed to an ecclesiology that sees the church turned inside out, the Carey movement (for Carey is now a movement with a few schools, childcare centres, church campuses and a large community centre) touches the lives of hundreds of families. Most of them do not yet follow Jesus, but find at Carey a sign of faith that is winsome, invitational and hopeful. And each year, more and more decide to follow Jesus.

There are many people to thank . . .

I am grateful to Lynn and Chris White for allowing me the use of their beach house in Albany, where I wrote several of this book's chapters. Some settings are perfect for writing. As I gazed out to sea, words flowed easily. Thank you, Lynn and Chris.

Then there are those who agreed to be interviewed at the end of each chapter. As with my earlier books, I have been concerned that readers should be exposed to some views other than my own. I asked Victor Owuor, Lloyd Porter, Travis Fitch, Yvonne Kilpatrick, Deborah Hurn, Dianne Tidball, Stephen O'Doherty, Rob Furlong, Phillip Nash, Becky Oates and Peter Christofides to answer questions related (directly or indirectly) to the content of a chapter. They have done so with openness and transparency, often risking vulnerability by their honesty. The book is so much richer because of their participation and I am so grateful to each of them for sharing their experiences and rich insights.

My wife, Rosemary, is ever supportive. Although her own career is rich and fulfilling, she always finds time to enter into my world. She spots what I miss, brings insights gleaned from the busy public hospital in which she works, and does so while ensuring that our home runs hospitably and smoothly. She is truly amazing.

I have dedicated this book to our three children, Nic (and his wife, Cat), Amy (and her husband, Aaron), and Jett, our youngest but now adult child. Each has found faith in Jesus to be life-shaping and transforming. They follow him joyously and obediently. They have enriched my life beyond measure, and they give me so much hope for the future.

Brian Harris
Vose Seminary, Perth
Australia

1

Jekyll or Hyde: More Than a Minor Dilemma

A Perplexing Problem

Robert Louis Stevenson's 1886 novella *Strange Case of Dr Jekyll and Mr Hyde* has remained popular well beyond any realistic use-by date. We naturally should ask why. True, the author was unusually gifted, and his other books continue to be published and read. More fundamentally, however, *Jekyll and Hyde* strikes at something deep within the human heart. Our shadow self, while not necessarily as blatantly awful as that of Mr Hyde, surfaces at uncomfortable moments, reminding us that we are not really the kindly Dr Jekyll we would like to project.

For those who need a quick reminder of the novel, it explores how there can be two personalities within Dr Jekyll – the one, moral and good; the other, Mr Hyde, totally evil.

It is always challenging when someone turns out to be significantly different from who you had imagined. I remember as a child being stunned to discover that my friendly and kind-hearted Sunday school teacher had been charged with shoplifting. Fifty years later I still shake my head and think, 'That's really hard to believe', but apparently the charge was valid – and not the first.

The problem works its way out in a thousand different ways. Some marriages grind to a painful halt with the shattering realization that the person married is radically different from the one idealized. In more reflective moments we might ask if the reverse could also be true. In that gap there is great pain.

At other times the difference might be spotted in the workplace. I now routinely advise people not to work for close friends – I have seen it sour so often.

Devastating though these problems are, they are not the major focus of this book. The particular Jekyll or Hyde quandary I seek to explore is the gap between what I would call 'toxic faith' and 'transforming faith'. Like many, I have come very slowly and reluctantly to the conclusion that faith – even the Christian faith, which is so precious to me – can be toxic. This troubles me deeply.

I remember my initial response to Christopher Hitchens' book *God Is Not Great: How Religion Poisons Everything.*[1] I wanted to simply dismiss it out of hand. It was too confronting, and so very, very negative. I still continue to believe that the book greatly overstates the case: no, I do not for one minute believe that religion poisons *everything* – such silly hyperbole. For all that, though, the book makes many sobering and valid points.

There is a real quandary that has to be faced. The growing antagonism towards religion is a trend we would be foolish to ignore. While we have become used to Marx's critique that religion is the opiate of the masses, and Freud's impatient dismissal of religion as illusionary, a new onslaught suggests that religious faith leads to ethically flawed outcomes. While in the past, atheists were usually content to justify their lack of belief in God's existence on the basis of largely *intellectual* objections, it is now increasingly common for the so-called new atheists to base their justification on *moral* objections. To quote the title of Hitchens' book again, it is alleged that 'religion poisons everything' and is in itself an evil. We might try to excuse this with the famous G.K. Chesterton paradox 'The Christian ideal has not been tried and found wanting. It has been found difficult; and left untried';[2] but a growing tide impatiently dismisses the sentiment as escapist and an inadequate justification for what they see as the poisonous harvest of religious faith.

While Christianity is not always the focal point of the attack on religion, it is certainly not excluded from it. Indeed, ten common accusations made against the Christian faith (in no particular order) include its complicity in:

1. Religious warfare
2. Colonial exploitation
3. Racial bigotry
4. The subjugation of women
5. Homophobia
6. The abuse of the environment
7. Retarding the progress of science – especially medical science
8. Academic censorship
9. Intolerance of anything new
10. Sexual abuse, especially of children

Clearly there is nothing attractive about this list, but it finds support in David Kinnaman and Gabe Lyons' study of the attitude of 16–29-year-old Americans towards Christianity. They noted six recurring images of Christians:

1. Hypocritical
2. Interested in 'saving' people rather than in relating to them
3. Anti-homosexual
4. Sheltered
5. Too political
6. Judgemental[3]

Again, the list is far from winsome.

Are we Jekyll or Hyde? What is it about religious faith that sees this disconnect between who we think we should be, and who we sometimes are?

The problem is not new. Consider Jesus' condemnation of the Pharisees and religious leaders of his day, found in Matthew 23. The language is harsh and strong as Jesus repeatedly calls them blind – blind guides, blind fools, blind Pharisees. The accusation of hypocrisy is also oft repeated.

Spare a thought for the recipients of the harangue. Contrary to popular belief, when your average Pharisee signed up for the job, it wasn't because he was desperate to be classified as a hypocrite. To the contrary, only the brightest and the best made the grade. The job requirements were daunting – being able to recite the first five books of the Bible by heart was just one of many. You can imagine a budding young Pharisee in his equivalent of a Sunday school class. The teacher asks, 'So who can recite Leviticus for us?' 'Pick me, Miss, pick me, Miss!' is the enthusiastic plea from all prospective Pharisee candidates.

Indeed, we don't understand the religious leaders of Jesus' day until we remember that there was a time when they were bright-eyed, idealistic and passionate in their commitment to God. No one else would fast or pray as long as them. Keeping all the law was more than a minor obsession. So how did it end in their being dismissed as blind fools and hypocrites?

Don Carson insightfully suggests that they allowed three errors to creep in.[4] Somehow trivia made its way to centre stage, while the really important matters of the law (which Jesus suggests are justice, mercy and faithfulness) slipped to the edges. And then there was the muddle between appearances and reality. Because most people are a little superficial, it became so much easier to ensure that things looked right, rather than that they were actually right. Closing the trio was the lapse into fussing about changing everyone's heart – everyone's, bar their own.

While this might have been their trio of errors, is there something inherent in the religious enterprise that is likely to see the most worthy of disciples eventually lapse into becoming a Pharisee? If so, what is it that makes religion an often dangerous enterprise?

Perhaps we are plunging into the negative too quickly. After all, the case for Dr Jekyll can be made. Let's acknowledge some of the positives that were accomplished by Christians in previous eras. It is only fair that we think of our achievements neither too grandly, nor too harshly. There is a glowing story of achievement that both can and should be told. Christians can claim credit for many of the positive social advances made in the last two thousand years. While multiple social factors are invariably at work in societal evolution, it is not fair to explore the abolition of slavery, the protection of the rights of women and children, the development of the welfare state, or the shift in focus from retributive to restorative justice, without repeatedly referring to the Christian faith that motivated and inspired most of those who championed these causes. And they represent a small selection of an impressive array of humanitarian achievements.[5]

There are also Christian leaders who inspire us. Who can doubt the wonderful legacy of St Francis or of Mother Teresa?

Not that we should limit our praise to those who have secured a place in the pages of history. Most of us know unsung heroes who have exemplified the very best of Christian faith. My mind springs to the youth leaders from my teenage years, a handful of Christian teachers at the local government school I attended, some courageous advocates for justice when I was growing up in apart-heid South Africa, and a thousand other godly people who in one way or another have convinced me that Christianity is not only an intellectually satisfying faith, but also one that has a compassionate outworking in the nitty-gritty of daily life.

It would, however, be simplistic to assume that the argument can be closed by referring to some of the more satisfying outcomes resulting from the interface between the Christ story and human history.[6] The shadow side must be wrestled with. There have been many times in the history of the church when it has been supportive of a right-wing agenda, which on occasion has revealed itself in racism, sexism, hom-ophobia, militarism, ecological and economic exploitation, cultural insensitivity and more.[7]

Again, this has not been limited to the documented periods of church failure and dysfunction. It has often worked its way out in unlamented stories known only to the few unfortunate enough to have been caught up in their development.

In my teenage years I was inspired by gutsy Christian opponents of the evil system of apartheid that had been imposed on the South Africa of my youth. I was equally perplexed and appalled by the many sermons I heard preached from Romans 13, where obedience to the ruling authorities is commanded in verses 1–7. This passage was applied as a blunt instrument, condemning all who dared question the obviously unjust and oppressive apartheid system. It was my first exposure to Scripture being used to justify the unjustifiable, but sadly it has not been the last. The one positive to flow from this was an early commitment to a questioning hermeneutic that was unwilling to be satisfied with trite and unethical answers.

I can also think of many more subtle examples where it was not possible to pinpoint something as obviously wrong, but where there was the sense that the Christian faith was being used to demarcate an exclusive society, entry to which was more difficult than that of the local golf club, and not as satisfying. While it is hard to articulate the precise contours of this, it often revolved around a 'them and us' mentality and an unscripted but not-to-be-departed-from set of subcultural expectations. The bottom line was always much the same. Those foolish enough to deviate from the script were simply not welcome and were excluded, not by muscular bouncers, but by a thousand looks and glances, whispered asides and non-inclusion in the spontaneous and non-formal life of the church community.

Again I must hasten to add that this was my 'sometimes' experience, not the daily fare of faith, and my dominant sense continues to be one of gratitude and wonder for the grace and love I have experienced from followers of Jesus the Christ. But this overwhelming sense only makes the opposite more puzzling. How can we so often be Dr Jekyll, and then plunge (even if only briefly) into the ugliness of Mr Hyde?

There are many dimensions to the answer, and we should not fool ourselves into thinking that it can be given quickly, dismissively or decisively. But it is vitally important to explore the question. Hopefully, as a result of more fully understanding the issues, we can limp our way towards an answer, one which must be given quietly and modestly, lest we fool ourselves that we could never again wear the mask of a Mr Hyde.

What, then, are some of these dimensions? Other chapters will explore them more fully, but here is a taste of some.

Intra- and Inter-Faith Differences

Christians are followers of Jesus the Christ. For most, this following is a result of a personal relationship with Jesus. However, it can't all be reduced to relationship. Faith is structured around a system of belief. And not all Christians believe exactly the same things about God.

The gap widens further when we consider those who follow the teachings of other faiths. While an oft-repeated mantra claims that all religions teach the same thing, it does not require too much investigation to establish the falsity of this assertion. For example, Jews believe that Jesus died on the cross and remains dead. Muslims believe that Jesus only appeared to die on the cross. Christians believe that Jesus died on the cross but rose again from the dead. Clearly each of these claims is different. If the claim was of little significance, it would perhaps not matter, but it goes to the very heart of the Christian faith. Jesus' resurrection or non-resurrection from the dead hugely impacts our conviction about what happens after death and the meaning of the Christian faith. In short, we cannot fool ourselves into accepting that the belief system of a particular faith is of no consequence, and that each belief system is essentially the same. It is simply not true, regardless of which definition of truth one adopts.

There are, then, two issues to be faced. How are we to deal with intra-faith differences, and how do we deal with inter-faith differences?

Intra-faith differences are those differences between followers of the same faith. For Christianity, this has historically been the debating ground between denominations. At times it has been very ugly. No one can read the history of the violence between Protestants and Roman Catholics in Northern Ireland and feel satisfied. While doctrine matters, it is hard to believe that it could ever justify the cruelty of the Spanish Inquisition. At a more ordinary level, it is tragic that until relatively recently the love between a Roman Catholic boy and a Protestant girl would often cause great alarm and bitter family division. Too often, the resulting marriage saw one or both partners having to abandon their family of origin. I know of cases where the rift has never mended.

Mercifully, denominational squabbles are not as frequent as they once were. Increasingly the diversity within denominations is greater than the diversity between them. I am a Baptist, and within my own setting I regularly come across Baptists who are proudly charismatic as well as those who firmly embrace cessationism. There are those who are best labelled Reformed in their theology, and those who happily wear an Arminian label. On questions like the ordination of women, some are complementarian, while others are egalitarian. Some are in favour of gay marriage, others are not. Some are young-earthers, others ridicule that position. Some embrace open membership in their churches, while others firmly exclude those who have not been baptized as believers. Some read the Bible literally, others talk about the meaning within the myths. In my adopted country of Australia, some vote Green, others for the Coalition, yet others for Labour, and still others for a range of smaller parties including those that are explicitly Christian. There is diversity everywhere, and any misguided attempt to place Australian Baptists in a 'one size fits all' box will fail. True, if you were to test each of these differences with a vote, one side would usually get convincingly more votes than the other – but fortunately we have not stooped to that. There is a maturity that means we don't have to blandly repeat a rehearsed party line, and most are able to delight in the variety of views. It makes it possible to explore issues thoughtfully and with the confidence that there will be others asking similar questions.

True though the above is, it is not a complete picture. Lurking not too far beneath the surface is a willingness to deflect back to a default drive of suspicion and dismissal. Labels can be used validly to describe a theological position; but they can also be used to caricature and exclude. Even when someone else's different label is spoken of politely, it can ensure that no meaningful relationship with that person will ever materialize.

In John 13:35 Jesus boldly predicts, 'By this everyone will know that you are my disciples, if you love one another.' At present, it seems hard to argue that this is happening.

Perhaps a thesis can be postulated. Christians are Jekyll-like when they explore their differences with interest, respect, curiosity – even wonder. They are Jekyll-like when they do not expect that the Christian faith will be parroted in exactly the same way by every follower of Jesus. They are Jekyll-like when they embrace the Pauline prayer expressed so beautifully in Ephesians 3:17–19, 'that you, being rooted and established in love, may have power, together with all the Lord's holy people, to grasp how wide and long and high and deep is the love of Christ, and to know this love that surpasses knowledge – that you may be filled to the measure of all the fullness of God'. This love, claims Paul, needs to be known *together with all the Lord's holy people.* There is a clear sense that when we are tucked within a cosy corner of faith, we can never fully experience some aspects of the love of God, for we are not exploring it together with *all* the Lord's people.

By contrast, Hyde is not far away when we use differences to vilify, caricature, dismiss or marginalize others. No, we don't need to pretend that we all see things the same way. No, we don't need to abandon doctrinal discussions lest we unearth some disagreements. Nor do we need to shrink from debate with one another. But we do need to remember that the one we disagree with is included in the togetherness of *all the Lord's holy people* if we are to more deeply experience the love of God.

But what about inter-faith differences? This is a more difficult question, but in this opening chapter perhaps it will suffice to point to the heroes of the faith listed in Hebrews 11. To state an obvious but often forgotten point, none of these exemplars of faith were Christians. To the contrary, they all died long before the birth of Jesus. Somehow, in spite of never having heard the name of Jesus, they lived as genuine people of faith and are recorded as noble examples who have much to teach us; as verse 38 notes, 'the world was not worthy of them' – high praise indeed. We will explore this a little more in Chapter 2.

Faith as an Opiate

While faith can inspire life's noblest journeys, it can also be used to deaden our awareness of the injustices on this planet. This was Karl Marx's complaint when he rejected religion as the opiate of the masses. Marx argued that while religion provided some comfort for ordinary people, it lulled them into a state of complacency. When you are not too concerned about what you receive in this lifetime because you have been convinced you will receive a better deal in a future life, you are more likely to passively accept what comes your way. In short, even though the present might be awful, the future is filled with promise, so settle down and patiently wait for the better day that will arrive some time after death.

Clearly, belief in a secure and happy eternity can serve as an analgesic and might so mask the pain of the present that there is little motivation to change it. The fact that Christianity has often been at the forefront of dynamic, dramatic and just social change shows that the link is not inevitable. The really interesting question is why faith sometimes leads to complacency and at other times to much-needed societal transformation. We explore this question more fully in Chapter 3.

Faith as Illusion

Freud is well known for expressing the view that religion is illusionary and arises from our infantile need for a powerful father figure. In addition he argued that religion historically helped to restrain the violent impulses of the id, which was necessary during earlier stages of societal evolution but can now be replaced by appeals to science and reason. Proponents of this view thus see religion as a defence mechanism against the trauma of our mortality. They argue that we draw comfort from believing that help is at hand from an external father figure, one to whom we are morally accountable – the latter belief helping to ensure that our behaviour remains within a range which enhances societal stability.

The claim is of course dramatic. It is no small thing to suggest that the religious experiences of literally hundreds of millions of people are essentially illusionary. Illusions can be very powerful. If I believe that a lion lies outside my front door waiting to devour me, I will routinely exit out the back door. Illusions can indeed shape behaviour. In addition, the undoing of an illusion can have powerful repercussions.

But is religious faith illusionary? Given that some religious beliefs contradict others, it is impossible that all can be valid and true. But that does not mean that all are illusionary. We should be careful of being too sweepingly dismissive. In addition, what are we to make of the fact that Christian conversion often helps people to face up to some of the deepest truths about themselves? As a result of conversion, many, many thousands of people have been able to acknowledge and conquer personal addictions, be they drug and alcohol related or from a vast reservoir of other obsessions and fears. Is this simply replacing one addiction (say, to pornography) with another (an addiction to Jesus)? Surely something more significant is at stake, and it seems inadequate and simplistic to label it as differing forms of illusion. There is much to explore in Chapter 4.

Faith as Poisonous

We have already alluded to Christopher Hitchens' claim that religion poisons everything. While it is easy to dismiss this as an obvious exaggeration, it is a claim Chapter 5 takes seriously, and indeed the argument continues to be filled out in Chapters 6 and 7. At times, faith is toxic. It is important to flesh out what tips faith into the venomous zone. Often it is about fanning fear into flame. The abuse of power is another potent poison, as is the cult of personality or an unthinking embrace of a utilitarian ethic that suggests that a greater good inevitably justifies an unsavoury means.

Some Ways Forward

While there are salutary lessons from poisonous versions of faith, there are so many expressions of faith that can and must be celebrated. Although this book is unafraid to name the disturbing, it is essentially a celebration of life-serving faith. And faith is so often life-serving. While there is much to be learned when things go wrong, there is even more to be gained from asking why so many things go right. We need to dig into the stories that give us hope and even a little pride. It is never enough to simply know what to avoid. There is much that we should embrace, and Chapters 8 to 11 move us into this territory. However, don't fall into the trap of glossing over the perplexing and disappointing, and don't refuse to read the earlier chapters. When faith encourages denial it will ultimately prove toxic.

On Not Defending Fundamentalism

Before we explore these topics in greater depth, a clarification is needed. Some versions of faith are far more likely to prove toxic than others. Let me suggest that fundamentalism is such a version. Most religions have a fundamentalist account of their faith, and Christianity is no exception.

John Stott suggested that there are ten telltale signs of Christian fundamentalism.[8] He argued that fundamentalists

1. Give the impression that they distrust scholarship.
2. Hold to an 'excessive literalism' in their view of the Bible.
3. Have tended to view the Bible's inspiration as a mechanical process. While theologians often speak of the double authorship of Scripture (human and divine), with the divine author speaking

through people in full possession of their faculties, fundamentalists have focused more on inspiration as divine dictation.

4. Tend to interpret the biblical text as though it were written directly to them, overlooking the cultural gap between the world of the Bible and today.

5. Are suspicious and usually rejecting of the ecumenical movement.

6. Have a separatist ecclesiology, with a tendency to withdraw from discussion when their specific doctrinal viewpoints are not held to.

7. Have an ambiguous relationship with the world. Sometimes values are uncritically adopted; at other times fundamentalists stay aloof for fear of contamination.

8. Have shown a tendency to cling to the myth of white supremacy and have defended racial segregation.

9. Have tended to view evangelism and mission as synonymous.

10. Are usually dogmatic about the future, often dividing history into rigid dispensations and going into considerable detail about the fulfilment of prophecy.

It does not take too much reflection to recognize that this combination of traits is likely to prove disastrous. In more extreme versions, there might be a justification of violence as a means to implement a particular fundamentalist conviction, though in fairness to your average fundamentalist, this should not be assumed and only occurs at the very far end of fundamentalism.

Fundamentalism lacks imagination. It finds security in certainty, which is nigh impossible to provide in the realm of religious claims. Rather than face the challenge of ambiguity, it takes comfort in caricatures and blocks out opposing points of view by distorting them. The irony is that the 'certainty' reached through this approach is extremely fragile. A narrow set of foundational assumptions usually undergirds fundamentalism, and if any of these are found to be wanting, the entire edifice is in danger of collapse. To avert this, an enormous amount of energy is expended in bolstering views that are usually unsalvageable. Whether through quests to locate Noah's ark or efforts to decipher a hidden code within the Bible, fundamentalists seek a shortcut to truth by oversimplification. Those who do not agree must be excluded, and it is here that the harvest of fundamentalism is often so damaging.

It is sometimes assumed that the opposite of faith must be doubt. More convincing, I find, is the counter-intuitive argument that the opposite of faith is certainty. After all, when we are certain of something, faith is redundant. What does faith mean if everything has been proved beyond the slightest shadow of a doubt?

I think the eleventh-century Benedictine monk St Anselm was right when he famously defined theology as faith seeking understanding. The quest to reach understanding involves curiosity, openness and creativity. It invites a rich dialogue with the biblical narrative, the history and tradition of the church, the experiences of believers from many cultures and many centuries, and the insights of contemporary culture and scholarship. It is an open-ended discussion, but not one in which anything goes. After all, as the discussion progresses, certain convictions start to emerge. Not that these convictions should be used as weapons to shut down any alternative viewpoint. Faith becomes increasingly convinced that some things are true, even while acknowledging that other areas remain perplexing. The tension is not overwhelming, but provides a welcome space for prayer, reflection and listening.

Faith knows that not every question will be answered and it delights in being released from the burden of having to pretend to know everything. There are many realms where we simply trust the goodness of God. Indeed, belief in a good God is perhaps the most basic building block for a faith that is life-serving and able to be celebrated.

In Conversation with Victor Owuor

To flesh out the ideas raised, and to ensure exposure to voices other than my own, I interview a different person at the end of each chapter.

Their stories vary, but each has grappled with what it means to be an authentic follower of Jesus – sometimes in very testing circumstances.

The first of these conversations is with Victor Owuor. Victor was born in Kenya and studied theology in South Africa, where he served as lecturer and dean of students at George Whitfield College in Cape Town. Victor is currently employed as the cross-cultural and indigenous consultant for the Baptist Churches of Western Australia.

Victor, you've experienced churches in several different countries. What differences have you noticed, and can you tell us some things you learnt from each setting?

One experience of church was at the Africa Inland Mission Station of Kijabe, Kenya, where I studied theology for four years. Abstinence from drinking alcohol, smoking and sexual immorality (among other vices) were considered important for the public expression of Christianity, while modest dressing for women was encouraged among those who served the different ministries in the station. Living according to the mission station's 'rules' could be confusingly used to define a Christian rather than having a relationship with Christ. Legalism has been confused for Christianity in many churches.

Conversely, many Christians in South Africa and Australia consider the above rules to be part of Western culture and not necessarily what defines a Christian. In some instances the Western culture is confused for a Christian culture or is considered to be a Christian culture. For example, if a Western Christian expresses the culture of individualism, it is considered a part of 'Christianity' that should not be condemned. However, every Christian community needs to have a biblical evaluation of how they express their faith in their surrounding culture.

To what extent do you think our faith is influenced by our culture? Are Christians just products of their culture with a religious veneer?

All people who become Christians get converted while living in a particular culture. Christ teaches that it is inevitable that Christians live in a non-Christian and sometimes anti-Christian culture (see, for example, John 15:19 and 17:15,16). However, they should not compromise their faith by allowing non-biblical elements of culture to negatively affect their Christian witness. Although there are positive elements in culture, Christians are vulnerable to negative cultural influences, but can resist them depending on their spiritual maturity. Christians can also play a transformative role in non-Christian cultures depending on their spiritual maturity.

Christians are not just products of their culture with a religious veneer. They express their faith in the culture they lived in before they were converted. Therefore, they enter into a lifelong process of applying their faith to different areas of life in society as they endeavour to glorify God in the culture they live in. Some elements of their culture will remain part of their lives while they adopt a new identity that their Christian faith represents.

Have you seen or experienced versions of faith that have disturbed you?

The most disturbing version of faith I have encountered is what is commonly known as the 'Prosperity Gospel'. This gospel's promise that all believers deserve good health and wealth, and that God gives both depending on one's faith, is unscriptural and can be damaging in many ways. Many Christians have fallen victim to teachings that are a reflection of a Western materialistic culture, which has subtly crept into Christianity and found fertile ground to germinate among the poor, the ignorant and the greedy.

When you think of healthy expressions of Christian faith, what examples inspire you?

Though many Christians have inspired me over the years, some of those that have been outstanding in my view are William Wilberforce, Reverend Martin Luther King, Eric Liddell and Charles Thomas Studd. Though none of these men were perfect, they were all convicted by the biblical truth that God could use them. They were opposed or misunderstood by many of their contemporaries, including Christians, yet they endured every difficult experience due to the godly convictions that spurred them to express their faith as they did. All of these men were inspired to express their faith in influential ways in history, yet did not live to see the immense impact that their faith represented. They all had a deep relationship with Christ, sought to glorify him and considered others better than themselves.

To Ponder and Discuss

Why not discuss the following questions in a small group, or reflect on them over time.

1. When you think of Christianity, do you more quickly associate it with Jekyll or with Hyde? Why?
2. Do you think there is any validity to the ten common accusations listed against Christianity or in the six recurring images of Christians noted by Kinnaman and Lyons? If so, what are the implications? If not, why do you think these claims are so often made?
3. In practical terms, how do you get along with Christians who see things differently from you?
4. Reread John Stott's ten telltale signs of Christian fundamentalism. Would you add to or subtract from the list? Do you think it is fair? Does it have any implications that you should take on board?
5. What do you think: Is the opposite of faith doubt, or certainty, or something else?

2

What about Other Religions?

Getting Going

This book focuses on what makes faith transforming – a wonderful life-serving force for good which is clearly to be celebrated. To do this we also have to look at the flipside of the equation. What sometimes makes faith toxic – something that drains life of delight and reduces us to being so much less than we were made to be? In this chapter I will focus on these two questions particularly as they relate to the interface between religions.

It would be so easy to stray from these questions. After all, when we ask about other religions we can rapidly veer into a debate on how to decide which (if any) is true. And let's be clear: religions do not all teach the same thing. Those who argue that they do have not bothered to consult the major teachings of each faith, let alone the finer points of detail. It really is not possible to reconcile the Hindu belief in reincarnation (and all that flows from this belief) with the Christian conviction that we live on this planet, die in due season, and then face judgement. And this is just one of a very long list of significant differences which could easily be drawn up.

Once we consult the small print, most faiths make some exclusive claims. In essence, it means that if one religion's claims are true, the competing but contradictory claims made by other faiths must be false. Logic emphatically underlines the impossibility of them all being valid.

For Christians who follow Jesus the Christ, much hangs on what we are to make of Jesus. While it is true that some faiths have been able to find a special role for Jesus – Islam teaching he was a prophet; Hinduism, that he was a holy man (in some versions of Hinduism he is an Avatar) – the status they assign to Jesus is still clearly a dramatic downgrade from that assigned in Christianity, where Jesus is the Son of God, a member of the Trinity. It is improbable that Christians will ever sit easily with this demotion, and this chapter will not suggest that they should.

The flipside is that there are real similarities between religions. The religious quest is usually birthed by a desire for something more – a transcendent other. Rudolf Otto describes the religious encounter as a '*mysterium tremendum et fascinans*', a use of Latin to help capture a sense of the God-mystery before which we both tremble and are fascinated, repelled and attracted.[1] There is a shared sense of wonder and mystery in the face of the God who is wholly other, and this is not the preserve of any particular religious faith. In addition, most religions have significant overlaps in their understanding of what constitutes an ethical life.

In short, while differences between religious faiths should not be denied, neither should the similarities.

But this chapter is not a discussion on comparative religion. We are not trying to score points for one belief or another, nor to rate the relative merits of each faith. Rather we will try to understand what makes faith a force for good – or for evil – and this especially as faiths relate to each other.

I will not pretend to enter this discussion neutrally. I am a Christian. Furthermore, I am a Christian happy to wear the 'evangelical' label – albeit one on the progressive wing of evangelicalism who veers away from fundamentalism. We all fit somewhere, even if it is into an 'I'm a new atheist, and I reject religion as poisonous' spot. Locating that position helps others to both understand and evaluate our place a little more objectively than when we feign neutrality.

Furthermore, although I am a theologian well versed in the Christian faith, I claim no special expertise when it comes to other religions. What I want to do, therefore, is not to champion aspects of any particular belief system, but to ask what it is about religious faith – of almost any variety – that makes us take a deep breath of satisfaction and say, 'No one can seriously say that that isn't good'; and what it is about some religious expressions that make us sigh and think, 'Oh dear' – and yes, sometimes the sentiment is somewhat stronger. More particularly, what is it about the interface between religions that leads to the positive and life-serving, and what sees it degenerate into the toxic? Likewise, what sparks helpful and hopeful intra-faith dialogue, and what does not?

Lurking beneath these general comments is the awareness that both the Christian faith and other religions have been linked to warfare and bloodshed. While I believe it is an exaggeration to suggest that religion is the cause of most wars, that is a conviction held by many. While this accusation is almost certainly an oversimplification (the quest for power being a far more pertinent driver), there is enough historical material to insist that we examine why religion can exacerbate the hatred between people.

When Faiths Encounter Each Other

When we encounter different faiths we are sometimes forced to face deep shadows in our own self. After all, all faiths do not teach exactly the same thing, and when someone suggests that our understanding of God is defective and that something different is required from us, it is threatening. It is the threat that flows from touching something that actually matters. Many things in life don't matter to us. If someone criticizes a musician or a movie I am not familiar with, I shrug my shoulders and think, 'Whatever.' It doesn't bother me. I have no real stake in the matter. But for those to whom faith matters – and for many it really, really matters – a neutral response is far more difficult. Sometimes it proves impossible, and can highlight some mindsets to avoid.

Here are some which might need to be challenged:

- *An attitude.* Succinctly stated, a common attitude is, 'I have something to teach you, but you have nothing to teach me.' Many of us have paternalistic mindsets. We are happy to instruct and inform others. We actually feel good when we do so. But the danger is that we see ourselves as the knowledge-holders, generously passing on our insights to those who do not have them. The flow is one way. We are the parents guiding uninformed and therefore unthreatening others. When we encounter people from other faiths, we are very happy to share the insights of our faith, but our eyes glaze over when the favour is returned and the suggestion is made that we haven't actually got it all right. We are more than willing to be the instructor, but are deeply unhappy if we are expected to be the student.

- *A need.* Many of us have a need to always be right or to always win. We have often been trained to be competitive, and we bring that competitiveness into every area of life. I saw it recently in an argument about eschatology that ended in a yelling match. I initially trained as a social worker, and as I watched the fracas unfold, the social worker inside me nodded with insight and said, 'This argument has nothing to do with belief but has everything to do with a need to be the one who is right or the one who wins.' Of course, the social worker in me could come to that insight fairly quickly because my inner theologian was listening to the argument with disbelief at the shallowness of each perspective. I was wise enough not to enter the fray. The need to be right sometimes shows up when we encounter people of different faiths. The fact that their faith is different is unsettling, because it forces us to face the question, 'Could I have got that wrong?', and if we always need to be right (and many of us do), this is a most unpleasant experience. We also often approach the encounter with a competitive mindset, 'How can I beat you?' being a default position.

- *A quest.* While the quest for certainty might seem commendable, it is helpful to remember that the opposite of faith is not doubt, but certainty. After all, if I am certain about something, faith is redundant. I need ask no more questions, and angst about the validity of my position disappears. I am right, and of this I am certain. But in the Bible, faith is the willingness to embark on the journey, not because every footstep is guaranteed, but because we are willing to trust the goodness and love of God. That does not mean that faith is ridiculous – a silly whistling in the dark – but rather that faith is actually faith. Faith is not irrational, but it will not be held ransom to the rationalist agenda that allows an ever-elusive desire for complete understanding to trump any other factor. When we meet with people who worship God in a different way, it can undermine our certainty, and so often people react to this.

- *A prejudice.* Sometimes religious disagreement is simply a thinly disguised mask used to justify and bolster our cultural and political prejudices. Entire cultures can be dismissed because they are seen to embrace a faith at odds with our own. It can also be a convenient way to find a scapegoat when things go wrong. Our prejudices also mask the limited way in which we view reality. For example, at a Trivial Pursuit evening I heard this question asked: Who first discovered the Victoria Falls? The answer given was David Livingstone, which was deemed to be correct. Well, it is only correct if you are sufficiently one-eyed to believe that there was nobody around the Falls until Livingstone arrived on the scene – which was clearly not the case. Thousands of years of earlier settlers could be overlooked because they were not 'of us'. Prejudice does that to people, and this kind of prejudice often operates in the religious realm. It can see us dismissing certain religious practices as being of little or limited relevance. A contemplative lifestyle might be quickly rejected as not achieving enough; a fixed liturgy might be regarded as uncreative and closed to the Spirit's guidance; while vegetarianism might be viewed with puzzled disbelief. At heart there are underlying prejudices that prevent us from truly entering into the world of those we deem to be 'other'.

- *A desire.* Life's most misguided quests usually revolve around the desire for power. An oft-repeated accusation from the colonial era is that 'while the missionaries read us the Bible, their government stole our land'. Sometimes the quest for power takes another route, and we marginalize others because they do not have the same religious views as we do. After all, what would they know? They worship the wrong god. Those who adopt an extrinsic approach to religion are motivated by what faith can achieve for them. At times, adopting a religious stance can lead to desired outcomes that have nothing to do with faith. For example, it is not uncommon for US politicians to use a religious ticket to win the approval of religious voters – often with no attempt at subtlety. The actual goal is political power, not the furtherance of faith.

To summarize, when we interact with other faiths, some ugly sides to our nature can quickly spring to the fore – our need to be in control, our competitiveness, our lack of real faith, our prejudices and our muddled motives. We can show ourselves to be people hungry for power, and uncomfortable in the role of learner.

This need not be the case. In better moments, interacting with other faiths, or with people who practise our own faith differently, can be deeply enriching. It can help us to

- *Embrace paradox.* Intriguingly, none of the exemplars of faith listed in Hebrews 11 were Christians. To the contrary, they all died long before the birth of Jesus. Somehow, in spite of never having heard the name of Jesus, they lived as genuine people of faith and are recorded as noble examples who have much to teach us. The Bible is filled with such paradoxes. The pagan city of Nineveh quickly responds to God's warning to repent. By contrast, Jonah, the prophet sent to preach to Nineveh, proves far more difficult to reach. It is the people of the other religion – not the prophet – who are responsive to God. Or consider the way in which Jesus makes a Samaritan the hero of his parable on what constitutes true love for the neighbour. You can imagine the muttering of the religious fundamentalists of his day at this provocative choice of hero. It is the person who would have been seen to be religiously flawed who wins the approval of Jesus.
- *Move beyond shallowness.* If nothing else, conversation with people of other faiths helps us develop an informed understanding of their faith and how it functions in the life of its adherents. The latter is important. We often think we understand another faith because

we have consulted a textbook or a blog post about it. While the information gleaned might be factually sound, it is only when we relationally interact with people of other faiths that we begin to sense what faith means to those who are insiders of the movement. This is about experiential knowledge and insight, rather than the ability to recite back the doctrinal tenets of a faith. Religion is usually something that deeply touches the heart, so a failure to grasp its significance at this level dooms us to only the shallowest understanding of the faith.

- *Challenge our assumptions.* In our post-September 11 world it has become easy to believe that every adherent of Islam is committed to violence. Islamic fundamentalism is indeed a menacing and disturbing force, but casual conversations with Muslim neighbours and colleagues at work will usually reveal a very different side to this faith – one that has nothing to do with bombs and terror. It is important that we allow our assumptions to be challenged in this way.
- *Disentangle culture from belief.* The 15 August 1988 cover of *Time* magazine was a mosaic of the face of Jesus built from portraits of Christ popular during different centuries. Each artist had captured a different aspect, highlighting something that was felt to be important during their lifetime. Some gave a hint of Jesus the sufferer, others of Jesus the mystic, king, warrior, judge, and so on. Each suggested a slightly different story. It is a reminder that the account of Jesus has been read in many different cultural and historical contexts and that to some extent what we understand about Jesus and highlight from his life is shaped by our setting.[2] The apostle Paul would probably be completely perplexed if he walked into a contemporary Christian church. It could be that he would feel as great a need to preach for our conversion as he did during his missionary journeys. So much has changed in the way we express our faith, and often this reflects our culture more than the essence of Christianity. Genuine dialogue with other religions forces us to disentangle culture from core beliefs. Sometimes when this is done the differences between faiths prove to be less than they initially seemed.

- *Ask if the faith of our birth is the faith of our heart.* It is no secret that most people adopt the faith of the family into which they were born. True, there are exceptions, when people intentionally renounce their family's faith, but a more common trajectory is for people to continue to attach some importance to it, but often with a lower level of commitment than the previous generation. As the generations pass, so faith fades, rather than being dramatically renounced. Encountering people of other faiths provokes us to ask if our faith is our own, or simply part of our loyalty to our family of origin. Though this process can be uncomfortable, it is profitable.

Perhaps you remember the thesis postulated in the opening chapter of this book: Christians are Jekyll-like when they explore differences with others with interest, respect, curiosity – even wonder. By contrast, Hyde is not far away when we use differences to vilify, caricature, dismiss or marginalize others. This is not to suggest that we should pretend to agree with things that we do not actually agree with. It is, however, far more helpful when a disagreement is based on an actual difference of opinion, rather than an assumed difference that flows from embracing a stereotype or falling prey to prejudice.

But the Bible Is Not Sympathetic to Other Faiths . . .

It is probably inevitable that someone will point out that, while we might congratulate faith on being Jekyll-like when it examines other religions with interest, respect, curiosity and even wonder, these are not attitudes displayed in the Bible. The faith of the Egyptians, Canaanites and Philistines is solidly condemned. It would be hard to credibly argue that the Bible advocates inter-faith dialogue. Indeed, the Bible oscillates between insisting on the complete separation between Israel and their neighbours (lest their faith and idolatry corrupt Israel), and urging Israel to be a light to the nations, wooing them to Israel's faith and lifestyle. Abraham's call in Genesis 12 includes the promise in verse 3 that, as a result of his call, all nations in the world will be blessed – so presumably some constructive interaction was envisioned.

Let's ask the hard question. Is the Bible itself part of the problem? If we lament religious warfare, what are we to make of the wars in the Bible – especially those which appear to be undertaken at the bidding of Yahweh and which seem to have a religious dimension?

It is as well to state some hermeneutical principles here. Just because the Bible describes something happening, we should not conclude that it met with God's approval. True, Israel was often engaged in warfare. At times Israel was the victor, at other times it suffered devastating defeats. Any reading of the Bible that suggests that God was uncritically on Israel's side must deal with Israel's many losses. Add to this the reality that Jesus was born a citizen of a nation conquered by the Roman Empire and suffering under its rule, and you quickly realize that the overall refrain when war is spoken of in the Bible is not one of gleeful triumphalism, but of loss and pain. That loss was often suffered by those who were identified as God's chosen people.

In my book *The Big Picture: Building Blocks of a Christian World View* I have written of the importance of reading the Bible in the light of its orienting passages.[3] Orienting passages are those parts of the Bible which give us a clearer idea where the larger picture is heading – the vision the Bible is building towards, which can sometimes be hidden by the messiness of the unfolding story. So, for example, if we allow John 3:16 to be an orienting passage, we heed its conviction that God loves the whole world and sent his Son Jesus so that anyone from anywhere in the world who responds to him can find the life that Jesus brings. This prevents us from reading the book of Joshua and concluding that God hated Canaanites and was uninterested in their deaths. In *The Big Picture* I speak of the significance of passages such as 1 Chronicles 22:6–10 and 28:1–3:

Ever heard people mutter, 'But the Bible is such a bloodthirsty book'?
On more than one occasion I have been asked to defend the moral vision

of the Bible, and particularly that of the Old Testament. The issue is the many corpses scattered across its pages. A quick reading could leave the impression that God is very one sided, caring about the Israelites, but having little time for anyone else. While the loss of Hebrew lives on the battle fields of the Bible is seen as tragic, Canaanite, Philistine and Egyptian carcasses don't really seem to matter.

1 Chronicles 22:6–10 and 28:1–3 give a clearer insight into the heartbeat of God. In these passages David explains that God had forbidden him to build the temple because the warfare with which he was associated excluded him from the project. For its time, this is radically counter-cultural, especially as ancient kings routinely built temples to thank their gods for military victories.

These passages are fascinating. After all, David's many military victories are attributed to God's help. David would never have defeated the giant Goliath unless God had made it possible. Why does God now decline David's services as temple builder? We must conclude that whilst God agreed that the brokenness of David's time required tough military action, God was unwilling for warrior imagery to be associated with the temple. In short, God makes it clear that warfare is a tragic consequence of human evil, and that it will never have the last word. Isaiah 2:4 imagines a day when swords will be beaten into ploughshares, and spears into pruning hooks. This is what we should long for and work towards. Jesus reminds us in Matthew 5:9 that it is peace makers, not peace breakers, who are the children of God. When placed in the impossible situation of having to choose between bad and worse, it is true that warfare was sometimes seen as the lesser evil, but to imagine that it is therefore God's ideal is to ignore the witness of the temple David didn't build.[4]

Not that it all depends on 1 Chronicles 22. Matthew 26:52 records that Jesus would not allow his disciples to use force to try to resist his arrest, and reminded them that those who lived by the sword would also die by it. Perhaps even more fundamentally, in Acts 1:8 Jesus alerts his disciples to the widening scope of their mission. They would be witnesses to him in Jerusalem, Judea, Samaria and to the ends of the earth. Converts were to come from every tribe and nation. As Paul was later to comment in Galatians 3:28, in Christ there is no longer Jew nor Greek, slave nor free, male nor female. The decisive divides from the past were to be done away with.

Until then, religion was most often a national affair. Each nation had its own god or gods and expected those gods to act in their nation's interest. Naturally, all wars were seen to be religious because the wars between nations were considered to mirror the wars between their gods.

As the early church built up a fellowship of people from different nations, a vision for something larger than the interests of a particular national group became possible. The missionary heartbeat of Christianity was always a call to embrace a larger vision. Bringing together people from diverse backgrounds and nationalities is a solid start in the journey to transcend national and cultural hostility. In the early fifth century, as the Roman Empire faced collapse, Augustine of Hippo (one of the greatest theologians of the church) thought through the implications of its demise in his book *De Civitate Dei* (*The City of God*). In it, Augustine argues that the message of Christianity is spiritual rather than political, and therefore rises above the artificial divides political interests try to impose upon it. This is a world away from the nationalistic warfare often described in the Old Testament. It is about a city open to people from every group and tongue. It is an invitation for people to pull together under a higher allegiance, rather than to pull apart because of language and bloodline.

But I Believe My Faith Is True . . .

Some might argue that the missionary character of most of the world's religions militates against religion ever being a force for unity or good. After all, isn't trying to persuade someone that our view of

God is right (and by implication, that theirs is wrong) inherently provocative? Does that mean that Christians disturbed by religious violence, and the harm that can be done when the religious differences between groups is emphasized, should renounce the missionary zeal advocated in the Bible? While some would say 'yes', I am not one of them. Here are my reasons.

I said earlier that I am an evangelical. I could also have added that I am a Baptist. Now, I would be the first to acknowledge that there are many things that my denomination has done that are wrong. However, there are also many fine parts to our history. One of the finest is that Baptists were among the pioneers of religious freedom. Their own history of facing significant persecution (and many early Baptists were drowned with the cry, 'If they want water, they shall have it') made them determined to defend the freedom of others who faced persecution. This was tested early in their history in New England, where they vigorously defended the right of the Jewish community to open synagogues and to worship freely.

No one who has studied the history of Baptists would suggest that they have been reluctant to evangelize or to embark upon mission. Indeed, their great commitment to mission is one of the reasons Baptists are one of the fastest-growing Protestant denominations. Somehow they have been able to hold in creative tension their real desire to persuade people of other faiths that the Christian faith is true, with a simultaneous respect for and determination to uphold the religious freedom of those they seek to reach. Not that older Baptists would have had difficulty in understanding this position. 'Convince a man against his will, he's of the same opinion still,' they would have quietly chanted if they were questioned about it. They deeply believed that faith was only genuine if it was voluntarily and freely embraced. If force or fear entered into the equation, it would always be at the expense of genuine belief. And it was only genuine belief that they were interested in. They ridiculed the idea of being converted at the edge of the sword.

In practical terms, this meant that when they were in positions of influence, they would work with other religions to ensure that members of those religions had the right to freely practise their faith. At the same time, they would never miss an opportunity to tell them of Jesus and why they were his followers.

This strikes me as healthy because it meets two key criteria.

First, defending the right of others to be treated fairly and with respect is taking seriously Jesus' instruction to 'love your neighbour as yourself'. Cited in Mark 12:31, Jesus in turn was quoting from Leviticus 19:18 – a lovely ongoing agreement between both Jews and Christians (and indeed Muslims, if we studied the topic in a little more depth). Respect for the other and commitment to their well-being takes seriously the biblical portrait that all have been made in the image of God and are, therefore, worthy of our esteem and able to contribute something to the greater good.

Second, while we must defend the rights of others, we also have to be true to our own convictions. If we do not speak freely of our own experiences of and beliefs about God, we are holding back from genuine dialogue. If we enter into conversations determined never to speak about the things that really matter to us lest we offend someone, we are not really present in the conversation, and are simply presenting a pretend portrait of ourselves. Such falsity is inherently unhelpful. So, to speak honestly and openly of our faith is simply part of transparent communication. Conversations are safest and most wholesome when what you see or hear is what you get. They are fraught with danger when genuine sentiments are carefully edited out of the picture.

Of course, the willingness to speak freely must be accompanied by an equal willingness to listen deeply. Just as we commit ourselves to honest and open communication, we must be willing to pay attention to the views expressed by the other participants. That means that we will ask questions to understand more deeply, rather than to try to trap and embarrass. While we will not pretend that differences don't exist, we will also listen for lines of continuity. After all, God's fingerprints are over all of creation. We should expect others to draw our attention to some we have missed.

What about Different Versions of Our Own Faith?

We have spoken about some attitudes that promote a life-serving faith in the interface between different religions. Much conflict has also been caused much closer to home, when different versions of the Christian faith come face-to-face. There are so many labels . . . Protestant, Roman Catholic and Orthodox; Pentecostal, Charismatic and Reformed; Fundamentalist, Evangelical and Liberal; Calvinist or Wesleyan – and so it goes on. Two thousand years of church history have seen much reflection on the faith, and many different nuances and emphases have arisen. At times, these have sparked violence and been the breeding ground for tragedy and resentment. At better moments, they have resulted in a more careful examination of the Christian faith and a richer understanding and appreciation of its many hues and textures.

Although one might imagine that the discussion between people of the same faith would be easier than that between people of different faiths, this is not always the case. Perhaps there is the risk that we take the goodwill of others for granted. We are sometimes harder on those who are close to us than we would be on others. Perhaps that is because we expect to disagree with people of a different faith or no faith. It comes as a shock when we disagree with those with whom we expected to agree. And indeed, when conflict arises it is sometimes easy to forget about the many areas that we do agree about.

Is there a way forward? Perhaps it is by taking seriously the promise of Jesus found in Matthew 18:20, 'where two or three gather in my name, there am I with them'. Remembering the 'plus 1' factor can transform conversations. At times, it sees us speaking a little less, and striving a little harder to hear the voice of the One in whose presence we meet.

In Paul's prayer recorded in Ephesians 3:14–21 Paul asks that 'together with all the Lord's holy people' we might grasp the width, length, height and depth of Christ's love for us (v. 18). The sense is clear. It is only together with all God's people (not just my like-minded little clique) that I will be able to begin to grasp the extent of God's love. When I realize the poverty of my aloneness and the inadequacy of my grasp of God's love, I become open to the riches found when I interact with others whose experience of God is a little different from my own. Genuine hunger for God will lead to greater openness to those who might carry a different label from mine. The solution to intra-faith bigotry and prejudice is a deeper hunger for God. This hunger will help us to spot treasures in the other that we otherwise might have missed.

In Conversation with Lloyd Porter

Lloyd Porter is the director of Operation Mobilisation in Western Australia and teaches missiology at Vose Seminary. He and his family worked as missionaries in Russia for fifteen years.

Lloyd, some people argue that the missionary attitude of some faiths, including Christianity, does a great deal of damage, and that all missionary activity should be suspended. What is your take on this?

I would have to agree that some missionary activity can cause damage, especially when those sent have mixed motives or are unaware of the cultural baggage their message is wrapped in. A quick study of the history of the church reveals that for the gospel to go forward, the cultural baggage has to be stripped away. For example, for the Gentiles to receive the faith, the gospel had to be de-Judaized. Later, the gospel had to be de-Romanized, and then around the time of the Reformation, de-Latinized. In our day and age, the cultural baggage of the West needs to be stripped away. That said, and despite the toxic faith and mixed motives of some, Christianity has been at the forefront of many amazing movements in Christian history that have brought about life and hope for many individuals and communities. I would argue that missionary activity should continue because, as we look at Scripture, we witness a 'missionary God' who does everything to restore his creation to a right relationship with him. We as Christians are called to be ambassadors of reconciliation and are given a command to take the gospel to the ends of the earth. As missionaries, we are to bring the message of the gospel, but it is up to local communities to make Spirit-informed decisions about the outworking of their faith in their own culture. Missionary activity must be about servanthood and love, and not about manipulation, force and power.

You work with Christians from many different denominations and cultural backgrounds. Are these differences divisive or can they be helpful?

We had the joy of working with the Russian Baptists in Siberia, who gave us a deeper appreciation of the cost of commitment as many of them had endured real suffering under the reign of Communism in the Soviet Union. The result of their faithfulness to Christ under times of severe persecution was a tendency to be very strict about dress codes, music, dance, drink and separation from the world. Many visiting short-term missionaries criticized these churches for their lack of joy and freedom. Yet for these Baptists, their faith was more centred on the suffering of Christ and a desire to abstain from the world and all it had to offer. Such strictness also helped their churches survive the years of persecution. After meeting a pastor who had spent years in a cobalt mine near the Arctic Circle under Stalin, my own understanding of commitment was challenged. His joy in Christ, his radiant love for the Lord, and the price he had paid for his faith were all way beyond anything I had experienced in my own life. The comment in this chapter about the *Time* magazine mosaic is correct in that many of the denominations and movements of the past have been inspired by one particular person or a certain context; they are valid responses to a loving God. That said, we must be aware that we often only have one narrow view of God and the mystery that surrounds the Trinity, and we should continually be growing and learning from the other communities that draw life from Christ. The Christian communion worldwide is a rich cultural tapestry with varied histories, cultures and preferences in worship which reflect the diversity of Trinity.

Do you think we have anything to learn from other faiths? If so, what are some things you have learnt?

Within the plethora of the world's faiths and belief systems there are many sincere and devoted people who are searching for meaning and understanding. Many of these devout people are willing to make sacrifices for what they believe. As I look at Russian history, I see that the Communists were just as willing to sacrifice their own lives for their dreams of utopia as the Christians were. In our Western world, I sometimes wonder if we have forgotten what it means to make sacrifices for the sake of the gospel. When Communism fell in the early nineties, 70,000 Jehovah's Witnesses went into Eastern Europe on short-term campaigns; the Mormons were also some of the best-trained missionaries in Russia – all of them trained in language at Brigham Young University. Where is our commitment and discipline? What kind of service are we preparing for? What cost are we willing to pay?

What key things should Christians remember when they talk to people of other faiths?

As we now live in a global village or city, we have the world's faiths on our doorsteps. We have many opportunities to engage with people from many different backgrounds, but that means that we have to cross a cultural divide to engage at a heart level. Jesus' interaction with the despised Samaritan woman is a helpful example of how we should approach people who have a different belief system. The Samaritans in Jesus' day were regarded with contempt, but they nonetheless believed in the first five books of the Old Testament. Jesus broke a cultural taboo to talk to a woman, treated her as an individual within her own context, didn't make gross generalizations about the Samaritans and spoke to her in everyday words that made sense in her culture. Jesus also addressed her lifestyle, but offered her hope and an alternative future. He made himself vulnerable in order to do so. As missionaries, we should be bringing a message of hope clothed in Christ's love, but it is up to local people to decide for themselves whether to accept or reject the message.

To Ponder and Discuss

1. Do you have a default attitude towards people of a different religious faith? If so, can you articulate it?
2. Do you find it difficult to speak truthfully about what you believe while being respectful towards alternative views? Do you think it matters?
3. Have you ever learnt something from someone of another faith? If so, what was it? If not, why not?
4. Think through some difficult ongoing conversations you are engaged in. How might remembering the 'plus 1' factor ('where two or three gather in my name, there am I with them') help alter the outcome?
5. Reflect on the sentence 'The solution to intra-faith bigotry and prejudice is a deeper hunger for God'. Do you agree? What might this mean in practical terms?

3

Marx: Faith as Escapism

Religion, the Opiate of the Masses?

Marx's critique of religion is famous: he said that religion is the opiate of the masses, or to quote more precisely, 'Religion is the sigh of the oppressed creature, the heart of a heartless world, and the soul of soulless conditions. It is the opium of the people.'[1] Not that Marx wrote a great deal about religion as such, and his critique of it should be seen as embedded within his overall critique of society. Whatever else Marx might have intended to say about religion and its role in society, he never wanted us to miss the point that religion can be used by oppressors to make people feel better about their lot, and thereby to render them tamely accepting of what they might otherwise have rejected. Religion is the spoonful of sugar to make the medicine go down – the problem being that this medicine is not for the good of the patient, but for the good of those making them take it.

This chapter is not an examination of Marxism but simply wants to explore the notion that faith can sometimes be used to validate an escape from this world, a retreat into irrelevance, rendering those who adopt it so heavenly minded that they are of no earthly use. Of course, one wouldn't naturally pick up on the fact that Christianity could be a vehicle of escape. Jesus' public ministry saw him actively involved in the woes and pains of everyday folk, and he never hesitated to confront the religious leaders of his day when he felt that their religious system imposed heavy burdens on ordinary people. In due course it led to his crucifixion at Calvary. Clearly this is not a model of escapism, especially when we factor in Jesus' insistence that his followers would, like him, have to carry their own cross.

For all that, accusations that Christianity can be a form of escapism are so frequently made that we must take them seriously. If even the Christian faith can degenerate into toxic irrelevance, what signs should we look out for to alert us that this could be happening, and how can we embrace a robust theology that safeguards us from this distortion of what should be? As an opening question, let's ask, 'Is worship escapism?'

Is Worship Escapism?

It is sobering to realize that the Bible itself seems cautious about the role of worship. There was no temple in the garden of Eden, and in John's vision of the future he assures us that there will be no temple in the new Jerusalem (Rev. 21:22). Genesis 4, which records Cain and Abel presenting different offerings to God, is the Bible's first record of an act of worship. Given that it leads to the first murder, it is a less than promising start. Much worship in the Bible is rejected as unacceptable to God, and invariably this verdict is linked to an exploitative lifestyle rather than to a liturgical oversight.[2]

But there is, of course, another side to worship.

I grew up in apartheid South Africa, and in those dark years often had to ask if worship was a form of escapism. Let me tell you of one example that remains with me to this day. I often ponder its many different dimensions.

Crossroads was technically an illegal squatter community, but its presence was usually ignored by the authorities as it provided a useful source of cheap labour for the city of Cape Town within which it was located. As the squatters' presence in the city was deemed illegal (even though they had been born in South Africa – but this was the madness of the apartheid system), they were a compliant labour force, unable to defend their rights or insist on a fair wage or reasonable working conditions. Any dissent, and their illegal status would be highlighted and they would be forcibly returned to the area of South Africa that the apartheid ideologues defined as their homeland – almost always an area with negligible work opportunities. In spite of the economic benefits of having an easily exploited labour force, from time to time the authorities felt a need to exert their power, and night-time raids would be ordered, during which, after minimal warning, squatter homes would be bulldozed. The resulting chaos was immense. Children were often separated from their parents, the elderly and infirm were at significant risk, and the meagre possessions of the community were senselessly destroyed. It was an outrageous breech of justice, and great suffering resulted from each of these raids.

A friend of mine served as a social worker to the people of Crossroads, sponsored by his local church – an exercise of prophetic faith by that Christian community. At around 2 a.m. one winter's night Paul[3] received a call informing him that a new raid had just begun at Crossroads and asking that he make his way there as soon as possible. Paul arrived on that cold, wet night to the sight of shacks that had been destroyed after only the briefest of warnings. People had grabbed what they could of their belongings and fled. The police and army had been called in to perform this atrocity but they had now departed, and the community was slowly regathering. Parents were trying to find children, community leaders were trying to ascertain who had been arrested, and weeping people were wandering around in dazed confusion. Then Paul noticed that a large group had gathered a short distance away, and as he wandered towards them, he heard that they were singing hymns – and singing them loudly and triumphantly. He was stunned. How could people sing hymns of praise to God at a time like this? A part of him was appalled. Though a deeply committed Christian himself, the last thing he felt like doing was singing songs of praise to God. His initial response was that this demonstrated that Marx was right. Religion is indeed the opiate of the masses, and at times of great suffering it mutes the pain so that victims don't protest as they should.

So he went up to the group and asked, 'How can you praise God now? Don't you see what has happened?' His tone was perplexed –

perhaps even a little angry. He says he will never forget the group's reply. One man looked at him in astonishment, as if he couldn't understand why Paul had so little insight. And then he said emphatically, 'Because they can't take God away from us. They can take everything else away, but they can never take God away.'

Was that escapism? Only to armchair critics. Those who have encountered life's most difficult seasons know that there are times when you simply cannot carry on unless there is something deeper which carries you. And to suggest that those who participated in the hymn-singing that night were indifferent to the struggle for justice is to insult the considerable role that the Crossroads squatters played in finally achieving the fair and free election which led to the demise of the apartheid system in South Africa.

This example serves to remind us that we must not be too quick to make judgements as to what represents worship as escapism, and we must certainly not confuse it with faith finding the courage to embark on the long and sometimes slow quest for justice.

Not that worship must always be linked to something as lofty as the transformation of an unjust society. Worship that helps to centre us, or that helps us to see the finger of God in an otherwise confusing landscape, is certainly not escapist. An old chorus suggests that if we turn our eyes onto Jesus, the things of this world will grow strangely dim. Perhaps. But I would suggest that if we truly turn our eyes onto Jesus, the more likely outcome is that the things of this world will grow strangely clear. Worship helps us to see life from a wider perspective, and so helps us to sense what really matters.

But it is not always so. Worship can also be about selfish self-indulgence, a passionate outpouring of petitions for personal blessing, or of sung commitments that bear no resemblance to the lived reality of our lives. The tunes help to anaesthetize us to both our personal woes and those of others.

Worship wars can see churches sidetracked into endless discussions about the appropriate volume of music, its style and its contemporary relevance – or lack thereof. When worship dominates the agenda, the church quickly forgets what it means to be church. Jesus' teaching to the woman at the well is always pertinent: 'Yet a time is coming and has now come when the true worshippers will worship the Father in the Spirit and in truth, for they are the kind of worshippers the Father seeks. God is spirit, and his worshippers must worship in the Spirit and in truth' (John 4:23–4). We should not be too quick to conclude that we fully grasp what it means to worship God in the Spirit and in truth – but we can be sure that when we degenerate into disrespectful squabbles about musical taste, we are far from what Jesus envisioned.

Sometimes worship squabbles bring out the best in us. I have met community after community where elderly saints have willingly set aside their musical preferences, recognizing that they serve as a block to reaching a younger generation. At times the favour has been returned.

Not that I want to suggest that worship is limited to the songs we sing. It is about our entire lifestyle. When we gather for corporate worship we bring the fruit of the week we have lived. It might over-flow into enthusiastic songs of praise, or after more difficult weeks, into prayers of quiet desperation. Many times it is simply part of the rhythm of our lives. There might have been nothing of particular note in the week, but we are people who have decided to follow Jesus the Messiah, and so we regularly gather to remember that commit-ment and to gain direction for the week ahead.

Is a Contemplative Lifestyle Escapism?

While for some the word 'worship' conjures up images of large crowds singing passionately, hands raised and hearts reaching out to the God beyond our grasp, for others the word suggests quiet reflection and prayer. It could take the form of thirty minutes of contemplation, or perhaps it is a larger commitment, a silent retreat for a day or two. At its most dramatic it might involve joining a religious order and dedi-cating oneself to a life of prayer and contemplation.

I teach at a theological seminary where I help students explore the Christian faith and its implications. Many of them sense that God has called them to be ministers or pastors, and wonder what this call might mean. During one of my lectures I show a documentary on the monastic lifestyle, after which the class usually enters into vigorous discussion. Without exception, some in the class will be dismissive of the vocation accepted by the monks and nuns. 'They are just running away from life,' they invariably say. 'It is good to pray – but you also have to be proactive, and set about answering your prayers,' others will comment.

Is a life of prayerfulness – a contemplative lifestyle – a form of escapism? In principle, it should be anything but. After all, the word 'contemplative' comes from the Latin *contemplatio*, which refers to the act of looking deeply into something. Its two Latin roots, *con* (which means 'together' or 'with') and *tempore* (the 'moment'), imply that a contemplative is someone who is deeply rooted in the present moment, fully alive to all its possibilities. Part of the alertness to the present moment is openness to what God is saying or doing in that space and time. Contemplation is thus about being fully present to God and therefore alert to the voice and instruction of God. There is nothing escapist about that.

Rather than contemplation being a form of escapism, the reality is usually different. When we reflect insufficiently on what God is saying and doing, we are more likely to use faith as an escapist crutch shielding us from the challenge of being fully present to God in the moment. Alternatively, we might be very willing to embark upon a course of action which we assume to be God-directed but in which we are simply following the whim of the moment. It is sometimes quipped that it is easy to mistake the good for God, and that the extra 'o' in good can prove disastrous. It is all too easy to impulsively dart off in a direction which superficially seems to be right. Waiting for a settled sense of assurance that we have heard the voice of God will help give us the strength to remain faithful to the instructions received.

But even the noblest path can have pitfalls. Can contemplation degenerate into escapism? Yes, it can. Wonderful though experiences on the Mount of Transfiguration are, the time comes when it is important to leave the mountain and go down to the waiting crowd below. As for Jesus and his disciples in the biblical account, the descent often involves returning to encounter the demonic and depressing.[4] There is no escape from the reality of living in a world tarnished by the fall of humanity. But a genuinely contemplative lifestyle helps us to become still enough to spot the lead of the incarnated Jesus who calls us to follow him.

Seven Risks to Watch Out For

Are there specific risks to look out for, signs that our faith is in danger of becoming escapist, perhaps even toxic? We will unpack many such risks over the coming chapters, but here are seven to keep in mind – one for each day of the week:

1. Assuming God sanctifies the status quo

Sadly, this is a trap we have often fallen into. It is easy to assume that what *is* represents what *is supposed to be*. For those who dislike change (arguably the majority of people), it is easy to presume that a passage such as Romans 13:1–7 (which at first glance appears to teach uncritical obedience to the government of the day) excuses us from seriously challenging the power structures of our time. What *is* must be God-ordained and therefore beyond question. If you happen to sit on the comfortable side of the power divide, it is very convenient to believe this.

Not sure what I'm getting at? Well, listen to these words: 'The rich man in his castle, / The poor man at his gate, / God made them, high or lowly, / And order'd their estate.' Ouch! This verse from the children's hymn 'All Things Bright and Beautiful' makes the point all too painfully. True, its author, Cecil Frances Alexander, published it in 1848 and had simply uncritically adopted the attitudes of over a century and a half ago. But it still rankles. Faith is never meant to complacently accept the status quo – a world where rich people are sheltered in their castles and poor people struggle at the gate. The religious leaders of Jesus' day would have loved him if he had adopted this line. He didn't – and crucifixion followed.

Not that it will always be as dramatic as this. Christianity and middle-class suburbia often seem to go hand-in-hand. Indeed, churches usually fare best in the suburbs, where a home, a mortgage and a few children, supplemented with the occasional exotic holiday, form the aspirations of the majority. And there is nothing inherently wrong with these hopes. But sometimes attaining these goals becomes a subtle form of idolatry. We need to at least be willing to contemplate the possibility that we might be called to something different.

2. Insisting that all things work for good

She was undoubtedly grieving, but it was her anger that struck me first. I was there to make the funeral arrangements for her mother, whom I had never met.

'Don't you dare tell me,' she hissed, 'that God works everything for good, and that my mother's death serves some greater good. There was nothing good about her death – nothing. She suffered terribly in the last few months. It almost broke me, watching her agony. I'm not sure the doctors really did their best. They said they did, but nothing helped. I would have ended it for her myself if I hadn't been too afraid of going to jail for it. What kind of a God allows this? And then my religious neighbour quotes some Bible verse at me, something about God working everything for good. If you come with that twaddle, I'll get a non-religious celebrant for the service.'

Amazing how Paul's sentiment in Romans 8:28 has been misused over the years. Here is what he said: 'And we know that in all things God works for the good of those who love him, who have been called according to his purpose.' This verse has been used to deny people the right to grieve: 'Why are you so upset? God knows what he is doing.' It has also been used to stop us examining our ill-considered plans and asking the penetrating questions we should: 'I know we can't see now why it all turned out so badly. But one day we will. God knows what is best.' It has been used to gloss over evil: 'I guess that really shouldn't have happened, but God will sort it out.' In summary, its misuse has denied us the right to deeply enter into experiences of pain, failure and disappointment.

Ironically, it is when we allow ourselves to enter that terrain that God often starts to work. Think of the many psalms of lament found in Scripture. Listening to them and praying them can help us to find some resolution for our struggles.[5] But some are afraid of allowing people to ask questions that might unsettle or trouble them. Sometimes it is because they would have to enter into the agony as well, and it is easier to escape by dismissing angst with a proof text from the Bible.

Joseph enters into the mystery of God's perplexing providence in Genesis 50:20. Do you remember his story?

Having been sold into slavery by his brothers, and then having suffered one indignity after another, his fortunes eventually turn and he is able to bask in the status of the most influential person in Egypt after Pharaoh. Confronting his brothers years later, he reassures them that he plans no revenge, for although what they did to him was motivated by their evil, God had turned it around and had brought good from it. The principle is simple but profound – what the brothers intended for evil, God had worked for good.

In many ways this is the Old Testament's take on Romans 8:28 (or perhaps we should say that Romans 8:28 is Paul's take on Genesis 50:20). God works in the midst of human evil and foolishness, and is able to bring about good. This is seen most clearly through the cross of Jesus. Who would have thought that good could come from that darkest of days? Yet on that day when evil seemed to have claimed its most decisive victory, God was actually working to ensure the defeat of sin, death and the devil. Yes, the Bible does undoubtedly teach that God can bring good from evil.

But there is a world of difference between this, and quickly assuming that everything that happens is right and exactly as it should be.

Joseph's brothers were wrong when they decided to sell him into slavery. Judas was wrong when he decided to betray Jesus. The crowd was wrong when they called for Jesus' crucifixion. Pilate was wrong when he ineffectually tried to wash his hands of responsibility for Jesus' execution. God is indeed greater than our sin and smallness. An old proverb says that God writes straight with crooked lines – and there are times when we see this. But it does not negate the sadness of many of life's scenarios. Yes, the long, painful death of that heart-broken woman's mother was sobering and sad. Only those unable to journey with the broken-hearted would try to prove otherwise. And quickly quoting Romans 8:28 to relieve us of the responsibility of making that journey is an abuse of faith.

3. Having faith in faith, rather than faith in God

I still get a little angry when I remember his death. He was a final-year medical student and had been told the hauntingly sad news that his death was only a few months off. His medical knowledge had seen him suspect that this would be the outcome, but like most people in that situation, he had hoped against hope. It was not to be. After some agonizing and angry weeks, something changed inside him. There was no more shaking the fist at God, nor any fear. Just a deep, settled sense of peace, and a conviction that God could be trusted, even when he was walking through the valley of the shadow of death.

And that lasted until a group of supposedly deeply spiritual Christian friends came and convinced him that God meant him to be healed. The reason this had not yet happened, they explained, was that he had insufficient faith. After all, if Jesus said that faith the mere size of a mustard seed could move a mountain, imagine how little faith was needed for a much more trivial miracle like the demise of cancerous tumours. The problem was with his faith. If only he would believe . . .

Why he fell for it, I don't know, but he did. I guess there is something deep inside most of us that feels a little unworthy – a horrible sense that we are getting something wrong. And we are at our most vulnerable when we are seriously ill.

Within days, the settled sense of walking with God through death's dark valley was replaced with a self-loathing and self-reproach. Why was his faith so inadequate? What a disappointment he must be to God because he didn't have enough faith to conquer his cancer! What would he say to God in the light of this failure? Indeed, could he even be sure that he would see God? Perhaps he would be forever barred from the presence of the one he had loved and served.

He died with that rampant sense of self-condemnation. And decades later I am still saddened when I recall what happened. He was fooled into having faith in faith, rather than faith in God. Faith in faith puts the entire onus on us. It is our faith that heals us, or makes us wealthy, or famous, or whatever it is that we happen to desire.

This theological distortion, articulated by Kenneth Hagin and then further developed by Kenneth Copeland and others, is sometimes known as the 'Word of Faith' movement, or more colloquially as the 'name it and claim it' gospel. There are many subtle variations, but in the end it boils down to a conviction that our faith can obligate God to perform the deeds we request. These deeds often revolve around our personal ambitions – our desire for health, wealth and happiness. Provided we have sufficient faith, what we request will happen. It is often followed with the proviso that we must make a positive confession that what we have asked for has been granted. Not too surprisingly, there are many testimonies to the effectiveness of this – though they should not be trusted. After all, those who acknowledge that they have not yet received what they asked for are blamed for not having enough faith, and lack of faith guarantees that the request will not be granted. As a result, people pretend to be healed or that they have had their problems solved – and often they believe their own deceit. It sometimes becomes quite peculiar. I have actually been in the presence of people who subscribe to this and have claimed, for example, that the cold they prayed to have healed has been cured – while they continued to sneeze over and infect all unfortunate enough to be in their close proximity. It might seem bizarre, but it is often tragic.

I remember talking to a man whose brother died of renal failure. He had prayed that his brother would be healed and, subscribing to the need for a 'positive confession', he proclaimed to all who asked that his brother was coming along nicely and that God was clearly healing him. As he said afterwards, 'I was so busy telling everyone that my brother was getting better that I never spent any time talking to him about his impending death. The one benefit of knowing that someone you love is terminally ill is that you can use the remaining time to say the things that really matter and that need to be said. I let myself be robbed of this gift. I can't believe I was so gullible.'

Why is faith in faith a form of religious escapism? Usually because it blocks us from facing the pain we are called to embrace. In running away from what we should hold close, we often run away from the God who wants to journey with us. After all, this is what the psalmist said in Psalm 23:4: 'Even though I walk through the darkest valley,[6] I will fear no evil, *for you are with me . . .*' (emphasis added). The biblical promise is not that we will avoid life's struggles and pains, but that we do not face them alone. When we close our eyes to the reality of what we face, we also blind ourselves to the presence of the One who offers to journey with us.

4. Settling for cheap rather than costly grace

In his classic book *The Cost of Discipleship*, Dietrich Bonhoeffer lamented that the Germany of his time had opted for cheap rather than costly grace. People wanted the benefits of faith but not the responsibilities that it brought. Genuine Christian community is hard to attain. To cite Bonhoeffer again, this time from *Life Together*, our dream of community is often at odds with our actual community, but it is our actual community that is the body of Christ. If we love our dream of community more than our actual community, we are at risk of becoming the enemy of the body of Christ.[7]

The task of working towards authentic Christian community is difficult. It is often easier to gloss over differences and to bury our own failures. But we are all broken people. Sometimes we don't care enough about others to challenge them or to query their comments and behaviours ('none of my business, really'). Not that I am suggesting that we should be busybodies, forever trying to spot the speck in the other's eye while ignoring the plank in our own. What I am saying is that we should care enough for the well-being and witness of the local church to genuinely get involved and to face all the struggles and difficulties that often result from this.

Clearly, it is easier to settle for cheaper forms of grace – attendance at a church that has my style of music and sermons with sufficient humour and irrelevance to entertain but not challenge. More significantly, it is an easier church community because I am essentially anonymous – my name known to a few, but little else. But this falls well short of the biblical model of what church should be. Genuine grace-filled communities are confident of the astonishing love of God – so confident that they empower people to face their deepest fears and their darkest secrets. It is costly to embark upon such a journey, but it is the journey that leads to authentic Christ-following. Ironically, it is cheap grace that turns out to be the costliest. Initially we are delighted to be lulled into the assurance that all is well. But no growth results from that path. We become pale shadows of what we have been called to be. That price is simply too high.

5. Sweating the small stuff while ignoring what really matters

Another way to embark upon escapist Christianity is to reduce the range of its concerns to the trivial. Micah 6:8 gets to the heart of genuine faith when it proclaims, 'He has shown you, O mortal, what is good. And what does the LORD require of you? To act justly and to love mercy and to walk humbly with your God.' The list is deceptively simple. It is not difficult to understand, but it is difficult to do. It is far easier to embrace petty forms of faith, those which focus on legalistic quibbles, rather than that which actually matters.

Trivial forms of faith abound. In the past they usually latched onto a small number of supposed evils to be avoided. It wasn't that long ago that the list included things like watching movies, dancing and drinking alcohol. Times have changed, and anyone arguing for a comparable list today is likely to be regarded as a quaint and irrelevant relic. For all that, the pull towards trivia has not disappeared. Many opt for celebrity Christianity, proclaiming their loyalty to distant preachers whose sermons they regularly download while ignoring the call to serve sacrificially in the flesh-and-blood congregation in their own location. It can take the opposite extreme, where attendance at every activity of the local church sees the window on the world reducing, as a very pleasant but essentially irrelevant Christian ghetto becomes all-consuming. It is easy for the local church to become inwardly focused, and when it does so, it usually develops disciples who start to think that raising funds to repaint the church complex trumps all other societal concerns. It is not that their concern does not matter; it is that it is too small.

Trivia also abounds when we uncritically embrace the individualism of our time. Church programmes sometimes revolve around helping us to feel beautiful and good about ourselves. The local church teaches us how to manage our finances, regulate our weight, avoid pornography and manage our family relationships. All this is healthy and sound, but if it is the limit of our concern, we have opted to escape into a Christian faith that equips us for comfortable suburban living. Genuine Christ-following usually stretches us beyond this zone.

6. Focusing on the letter of the law, rather than the motivation behind it

The religious leaders of Jesus' time were experts at this. Knowing the instruction to tithe their income, they carefully counted the number of mint leaves in their garden, and added the tally to their calculation of the tithe due (Matt. 23:23). Their diligence would have been commendable if it hadn't so consumed their energy that it left them with little time for anything else. They fell into the trap in other ways. Knowing that obedience to the Sabbath laws was a way to honour God, they protested when Jesus performed a miracle on this sacred day. After all, it was not a day for work – and miracles, while unusual, presumably fell into the category of work (John 5:1–18).

It is easy to use the Bible as a blunt instrument, quoting its verses outside of their historical and cultural context, and tritely assuming an automatic correspondence between those times and our own. When we do so, we sometimes miss the heartbeat behind the passage. Take, for example, Genesis 1:28a, where God speaks to the recently created Adam and Eve: 'God blessed them and said to them, "Be fruitful and increase in number; fill the earth and subdue it."' A literalist would note the instruction to increase in number and fill the earth, and conclude that any form of birth control should be banned. After all, if God has instructed us to be fruitful and to expand our numbers, how can we justify taking steps to restrict our expansion? By contrast, those who dig a little deeper quickly note that the instruction was given at a time when the earth was sparsely populated. It is one of the few biblical commandments that have been obeyed. A world of seven billion people is a very different world from that faced by Adam and Eve. Paradoxically, the way to be 'fruitful' now requires us to be less fruitful in a literal sense. To fulfil the intent of this passage, we now need to have smaller families, not larger ones. Context matters, and insensitive readings of the biblical text are unhelpful.

We must be willing to ask the 'why' question of Scripture. This is the instruction – but why? Unpacking the 'why' helps us to build a world view that will stretch and challenge us. It is not a task for escapists.

7. Trivializing eschatology[8]

For many, thoughts about the return of Jesus revolve around leaving this planet for heaven. The world becomes a place to leave, not a place to strive for and protect. A flawed eschatology lies behind this.

Much of our thinking about the 'end times' has been reduced to unseemly debates about millennialism. Though most churches no longer require you to affirm whether you are premill, postmill or amill (and indeed, the fascination with millennialism has disappeared in most circles), an apocalyptic escapism is often close to the surface. In crassly reductionist terms, the world and everything in it is to be destroyed, so why bother to build a better world if destruction is simply around the corner? In one rather extreme example of bad theology, a pastor is alleged to have urged his congregation to do all they could to degrade the environment, claiming that the chaos caused by pollution and global warming would hasten the return of Christ. While it would be unfair to suggest that such views are typical, an emphasis on the destruction of the present planet is unlikely to see a flurry of activity to ensure its well-being.

A closer examination of the biblical text suggests that what we actually await is the creation of a new heaven and a new earth. The title 'a new earth' is suggestive. It is the retention of the word 'earth' that is so especially interesting. Whatever the future holds, the concept of the 'earth' does not disappear. It will indeed be renewed – a *new* earth – but it will not be so discontinuous from the old that a new name is required. It is still *earth*.

Indeed, in Revelation 21 John has a vision in which he sees the merging of the realms of heaven and earth as the new Jerusalem comes down out of heaven to the new earth. The cry in verse 3 is 'Look! God's dwelling-place is now among the people, and he will dwell with them.' Perhaps this is why Jesus urged us to pray 'Your kingdom come, your will be done, on earth as it is in heaven', to cite Matthew 6:10. Just as God's will is carried out in heaven, so it should be carried out on the earth. If, therefore, we want to know how we should act on earth, we should ask, 'How is this done in heaven?' Rather than the standard of heaven being an inaccessible one delayed until the end of all things, Jesus instructs his followers to pray for the strength to implement that agenda in the present. There is nothing escapist about this.

Stanley Grenz and John Franke have suggested that we view eschatology as our orienting motif in theological construction.[9] By this they mean that we should allow our convictions about the nature of our future reality to shape and direct, indeed to orientate, our present actions. Rather than eschatology becoming about escapism, it shapes our current agenda. Our vision of the future shapes the now. In 1 Corinthians 13:13 Paul reminds us that the three things that will remain for ever are faith, hope and love, with love being the greatest. What projects should we enthusiastically endorse in this present age? Those that flow from and reflect faith, hope and love, for they will remain for ever. If this sounds escapist to you, escapism is not what it used to be.

While there may be times when it is appropriate for the Christian faith to shield us from reality, to be an opiate helping to alleviate the unbearable suffering of the present, this is not the usual role faith plays in the lives of those who follow Jesus the Messiah. More commonly, our faith and trust in Jesus gives us the confidence to face the challenges of our time and to follow Jesus in serving the world he loved and died for. The only escape that the Christian faith offers is an escape from the superficiality of our times. And that is an escape worth making.

In Conversation with Travis Fitch

Travis Fitch has worked as a pastor and is currently the CEO of 12 Buckets, a not-for-profit organization based in Perth, and which he founded.

What does healthy faith look like for you?

For me, a key element of healthy faith is, as one friend described it, *resurrection faith*. Resurrection faith is that aspect of faith that can only be refined either as death hangs on the horizon or as we find ourselves unexpectedly plunged into its turbulent waters.

Healthy faith, or, in this case, resurrection faith, sings out in the tradition of the Apostles' Creed, 'I believe in the resurrection', despite being in the face of circumstances that stretch us to the point where we're looking to reach for rage, resignation or self-medication.

When *that* person, relationship, dream, ability or point of safety has died or looks to be under threat of no longer being a presence in our lives, resurrection faith enables us to continue walking in the way of love as the Spirit affirms over again that we are for ever one with Jesus Christ – the one who holds together the old world and the world to come, the one through whom God is making all things new.

There came a point in 2013 when it looked as if 12 Buckets could fold. Funding is always tight for not-for-profits, but we had just four months to turn things around before money ran out and, very quickly, sixteen weeks became five. I knew the Lord had placed the concept of 12 Buckets in our hearts, but I also knew that what was built could still come to an end. I came to the point where I decided to begin any answers to enquiries about how 12 Buckets was going with, 'Well, I believe in the God of the resurrection.' For me this was a statement that said, 'This may all fold, but because the Lord burned into our hearts the needs of disadvantaged children, we are sure he will bring something more glorious to life.'

You've experienced some unhealthy versions of faith. What went wrong?

In short, what went wrong was a real-life retelling of Jesus' parable about the religious leader and the tax collector (Luke 18:9–14) or his diagnosis of Plank-Eye Syndrome (Luke 6:41–42). 'Thank God I'm not like them . . .'

In my case, it was the church's cold response to my parents' divorce – though by Dad's admission he had responded similarly to others' divorces before his and Mum's marriage broke down. That said, I remember, as a 12-year-old, feeling the relational wintriness on an occasion when Dad and I returned to a church service one particular Sunday. Of course, while people appearing to struggle to even offer eye contact could have been due to mere awkwardness, I'm sure it is a grounded assessment that this was judgement on their part, and I certainly left that day with a clear impression that we did not belong.

The church, for the most part, seems to have got its head around how to be more pastoral and gracious with this kind of relational breakdown. I know numerous people who, despite marriage breakdown, continue to have a sense of place in their church communities. These are churches that, far from championing divorce, seem to have greater grace for recovering sinners.

Today, I believe the pressing question that needs more open and gracious consideration is not around divorce, but how we will welcome LGBTI Christians into our church communities – and by 'welcome' I do not mean 'tolerate'. If we have not done so already, is it not time for us to eat with, share life with, serve alongside and worship with brothers and sisters who are LGBTI? How will we join together, acknowledging *our collective need* for wholesale restoration?

In what ways have you sometimes contributed to the toxicity?

I have condemned and I continue to condemn. I am a recovering sinner who hopes that, by the time he is 80, he is by God's grace contributing far less anti-kingdom toxicity to his family and community by means of condemnation.

To be candid about one area, while I hope I actively care about issues of justice in a way that goes beyond tweets and status updates, I am also aware that in my heart I have condemned people who I have perceived to be less concerned about what happens to 'the least of these'.

'Thank God I'm not like them . . .'

I express this anti-kingdom toxicity in a few ways, but probably most regularly by being unhelpfully provocative and argumentative. I have developed somewhat of a knack for getting a rise out of people and then painting them into a corner with ferocity masked by 'pious concern for the issue at hand'. Of course, there are times when debate is right and passion is appropriate, but when they replace genuine love for the person I am speaking to with the proverbial judge's gavel, my heart is no longer in alignment with Christ's.

Upon reflection, I believe it is critical that I (and we) remain aware that any matter of importance in relation to Christ and his church will be held and delivered with a sense of toxicity; be it the distortion of the past, the well-travelled roads of our prejudice and the blind spots I'm sure we all carry.

So we must pray, 'See if there is any offensive way in me, and lead me in the way everlasting' (Ps. 139:24).

Tell us about 12 Buckets and how it helps you to serve God more fully.

At 12 Buckets, we want to see all children flourish regardless of their background or circumstances. 12 Buckets is made up of people who are committed to supporting disadvantaged and at-risk primary-aged children. We currently do this in Perth's northern suburbs – specifically Balga and Koondoola. We offer our programme within primary schools during school hours, so as to encourage school attendance and engagement. The foundational concept is pretty simple: schools refer children who need academic or socio-emotional support to 12 Buckets. We then work collaboratively with the school to try to unearth that child's existing area/s of strength, and we then create a tailored module of learning that develops that area of strength or interest while targeting the academic and socio-emotional needs.

The decision to structure as a non-religious organization was important for us. As an advocate of common grace, were I to wire a specifically Christian charter into our service I would have cut us off from sharing, serving and learning from others who have been beautifully gifted by God – whether they acknowledge him as the giver of their talents or not.

While we do not discuss religious or spiritual content with the children we help, because 12 Buckets is so inextricably linked to my own formation story, I have found the Lord using it as a catalyst to conversation with a wide range of people about the 'Unknown God'. In this sense, along with being part of something that is meaningfully helping vulnerable children, I love the opportunities that come to talk about the roots of it all – for I believe 12 Buckets too was created in Christ Jesus (Eph. 2:10).

To Ponder and Discuss

1. Reflect on the worship at your local church. Does it motivate you to serve God more fully, or is it an escape from reality?
2. Reflect on the seven warnings that faith is at risk of proving escapist:

   - Assuming God sanctifies the status quo
   - Insisting that all things work for good
   - Having faith in faith, rather than faith in God
   - Settling for cheap rather than costly grace
   - Sweating the small stuff while ignoring what really matters
   - Focusing on the letter of the law, rather than the motivation behind it
   - Trivializing eschatology

   Do you relate to any of them? Do you need to make any changes?
3. What do you think of the statement 'Ironically it is cheap grace that turns out to be the costliest'? What does this mean? Can you think of some times when this has turned out to be the case?

4

Freud: Faith as Illusion

A Father Christmas Faith?

If for Marx, faith is escapist, for Freud, it is illusionary. In *The Future of an Illusion*, Freud (1856–1939) dismisses religion as 'a universal obsessional neurosis of humanity' and claims that 'a turning-away from religion is bound to occur with the inevitability of a process of growth'.[1] Not that all psychologists agree with Freud. A notable exception was Swiss psychotherapist Carl Jung (1875–1961), who 'concluded that a spiritual attitude was an essential of human life and that the development or recovery of a religious outlook was the prime determinant of psychological health'.[2] Clearly Freud's argument has not been accepted uncritically in the wider arena, but his assumption that religion is illusionary is cited so often that it is important that we examine it.[3]

Is our faith a pleasant fairy tale, a childlike longing for Father Christmas? In the face of our vulnerability, experienced so powerfully in infancy, do we simply create a fantasy father figure and call him God – a being who will protect us from our powerlessness? Are all our unresolved and unattainable wishes, like life after death and being re-united with loved ones, imaginarily solved by this self-created illusion? While arising from our own inner fears, is the illusion reinforced by our broader culture which, facing similar fears, lauds the worthiness of the myth, and continues to perpetuate it? If this is the case, religion clearly holds us back from facing the truth of our existence – whatever that truth might be.

The debate moves us well outside the realm of psychology, and a full investigation would require us to examine the apologetic arguments in defence of the Christian faith. If Christianity is true, it is not an illusion, regardless of whether psychological factors make it attractive or not.[4] A strong case can be made for the rationality of belief both in God in general and in the Christian God in particular. Following this fascinating red herring would move us beyond the scope of this chapter, but I have included some helpful references in the footnote[5] for those who would like to read further on this topic.

As in the previous chapter, where reference to Marx was a springboard to facilitate an exploration of escapist versions of faith, I will not embark upon a serious exploration of Freudianism but rather will use Freud to examine the idea that toxic faith can be a way of avoiding reality and can shelter people from a genuine quest for truth.

The illusionary aspects of toxic faith can be many-faceted. We can start to build imaginary and unhelpful worlds that are filled with outsiders with whom we dare not relate lest they contaminate us and our beliefs. This can block us from seeing the humanity in others, and can limit our involvement in the world. Following an illusion can see us reject many of life's options before we have even really considered them. It can justify a numbing of the intellect, especially when its insights prove threatening or challenge cherished but vulnerable notions. These traits are especially notable in religious sects, but more modest versions sometimes operate in local church congregations which slowly but surely isolate their members from their broader community. A 'them and us' mentality often accompanies religious faith.

The illusionary can also move in a different direction, where we delude ourselves that we are the centre of God's plan for the world and that astonishing things will flow from our obedience. While this is often a harmless and sometimes even motivating myth, we should question the egocentric assumptions behind so many prophecies that declare that a particular local church will be the launching pad for world revival, and that every person in our group must be destined to change the world. These over-the-top predictions usually flow from our need to feel important, rather than from the plans and purposes of God. They are illusions to make us feel better about what is probably our more ordinary lot in life. A reluctance to embrace the wonder and beauty of everyday life often lies behind our quest for something dramatically different. The price tag is that we fail to see the wonder of what is, because we are always hungry for something else.

To begin our exploration, it is helpful to consider different kinds of religious orientation.

Extrinsic, Intrinsic and Quest Religious Orientations

American psychologist Gordon Allport (1897–1967) was a pioneer in the field of personality theory and of trait theory in particular. He differentiated between internal and external forces at work within an individual, calling these forces genotypes and phenotypes. Your genotype is an internal force and refers to the way in which you retain information and use it to interact with the world. Your phenotype is an external force and denotes the way in which you relate to your surroundings and to forces external to you as an individual. According to Allport, the interaction between these forces (genotype and phenotype) shapes behaviour, and forms the basis for the individual traits which differentiate people from each other.

Allport uses these basic observations to help develop his views on religion, in which he distinguishes between extrinsic and intrinsic religious orientations.[6]

Those with an extrinsic religious orientation view religion as a means to an end, and will often use it to achieve non-religious goals. The motivation is frequently selfish and is about what the individual can get as a result of their religious affiliation. In the era of Christendom, when the Christian faith dominated the social landscape, extrinsic religious motivation was common. People had a great deal to gain by their religious membership, and a church reference would often bolster a job application or help to ensure the success of a request to rent a property.

We now live in a post-Christendom era in which there is usually little to gain by being associated with the Christian faith (in fact, the reverse is now often true), so extrinsic religious motivation is currently less common. Interestingly, Allport found a correlation between extrinsic religious motivation and prejudice.[7] Perhaps this is why in the era of Christendom the church often found itself on the side of oppressors, while in a post-Christendom era it is more likely to speak with a prophetic voice.

Allport contrasts an extrinsic orientation with an intrinsic one, and claims that those with an intrinsic religious orientation view their religion as an end in itself. The person sincerely believes their creed and seeks to live in the light of it. Their faith is usually the most important part of their life, and is seen as a valid end in itself. In other words, the adherent is not seeking to gain anything from their religion; their reward is in faithfully following its teaching. Allport found that an intrinsic religious orientation is negatively related to prejudice – though more nuanced presentations of this view point out that it depends on what the religion actually teaches about an issue. So if the religion is prejudiced against a particular group or behaviour, an intrinsic follower is likely to demonstrate that same quality.

While differentiating between extrinsic and intrinsic religious motivations has dominated the landscape for the last half century, the concept is now usually expanded to include Batson's concept of a quest religious orientation.[8]

Those with a quest religious orientation view religion neither as a means nor an end, but as a quest for truth. While they recognize that truth may never be found, questions are considered important and the quest for truth remains open ended. By definition, quest religious orientations are not related to prejudice as they require an open questing, rather than a prejudiced unwillingness to explore.

As with all trait theories, we need to recognize the danger of reductionism (it is never really as simple as that) and that pure traits rarely exist. In other words, we should think of dominant traits, rather than exclusive traits. Even those with an essentially intrinsic orientation will at times be driven by extrinsic concerns, as, for example, when a dedicated and sincere church family decide to leave their local church because they are concerned that it is not meeting the spiritual needs of their teenager. Their desire to have their adolescent embrace the faith turns them into consumers, carefully comparing the strengths of different church youth programmes. If it had only been up to the parents, they would probably have stayed, but faced with the likelihood of their son or daughter rejecting the faith, different priorities start to dominate.

Likewise, we should not assume that those who are essentially extrinsically orientated have no personal convictions; and both intrinsically and extrinsically orientated people are sometimes driven by a quest to seek a deeper level of truth.

The average church congregation is made up of people of all three of these religious orientations, and the interaction between them can prove stretching. I am part of the evangelical community, and I recognize that evangelicals are usually comfortable with those of an intrinsic orientation but often battle to understand those guided by a questing disposition. Their quest for truth is often misunderstood, as evangelicals often assume they have already found it and struggle to accept that the quest for truth needs to continue.

Ironically, in their passionate desire for church growth evangelicals often pander to those with an extrinsic motivation – the religious consumers of our age who will only attend a church if the music, youth programme and building are to their liking. They are then perplexed that the faith of those recruited seems to be shallow and is easily abandoned.

What has this to do with faith as an illusion? Perhaps it alerts us that there are various religious motivations. Freud overgeneralizes, and misses the range and complexity of the religious quest.

In addition, in our search for life-serving faith it is helpful for us to speak words of encouragement to certain religious motivations. Intrinsic faith is commendable. It is genuine and heartfelt. It is deeply enriched when accompanied by an ongoing quest for deeper levels of truth. Rather than being dismissive of those who continue to ask questions, we should embrace them as followers of the one who described himself not only as the way and the life, but also as the truth (John 14:6). The search for truth eventually leads to the insight that truth is best found in relationship – primarily relationship with Jesus, in whom, to cite the apostle Paul, 'all things hold together' (Col. 1:17). Rather than dismissing as lacking belief those who continue to question, we should recognize that for those of a quest orientation, questioning is part of the essence of faithful belief.

This is often shown in the differing attitudes to the Bible adopted by those of intrinsic and quest orientations. For the intrinsic, the Bible says it, and that settles it. Our task is to find a way to faithfully implement its teaching. Clearly this will not do for those of a quest orientation. They will want to know why the text says what it does, and will keep probing the motivation behind it. They are unlikely to give the Bible their unquestioning allegiance, but equally, they will not dismiss it out of hand. They will interrogate and investigate it. Interestingly, new insights into the biblical text are therefore more likely to be found by those of a quest orientation than by those who are intrinsically motivated.

While it will be clear that I am the least enthusiastic about extrinsic forms of faith, those with this orientation also have their role to play. They help to ground us in the reality of day-to-day life. Their concern is usually pragmatic. 'Does it work and will it help me?' is their bottom line. These are realistic questions that should not be overlooked.

But have we answered the 'Is faith an illusion' question? There is another dimension to look at, and that is the explanatory power of the Christian metanarrative.

The Explanatory Power of the Christian Metanarrative

Christianity is a metanarrative and needs to be evaluated by its explanatory power. In other words, Christianity does not claim to simply be one story among many, but to be a story which ultimately makes sense of all stories. Does the world make sense if we live in the light of this story? If it does, Christianity is not illusionary but is an exercise in healthy sense-making. Christianity is a lens through which we can view the world; it is a world view. If when we look through this lens things which otherwise seem senseless start to fit together, we have an account of reality which must be taken seriously. It has explanatory power, and might therefore be true.

What, then, is the Christian story, and does it provide a convincing and life-affirming account of reality – an account large enough to make sense of all the differing stories that make up the mosaic of life? While I will answer this question more fully in Chapter 7, at this stage I would like to focus on some aspects of the Christian metanarrative that point us towards active, practical and constructive engagement with this world. If tangible and helpful things flow from this system of belief, it is hard to dismiss it as an illusion to protect us from the less palatable dimensions of life.

Jesus commanded us to follow him, and not by the wildest stretch of the imagination could his journey be described as wishful, irrelevant, sheltered or detached from the harsher realities of life. Indeed, if Freud is right and religion is an illusion to protect us from facing the threats of life, it is difficult to understand how the Christian faith was ever birthed. Its founder was crucified, and his early followers faced significant persecution. Embracing Christianity requires us to take a walk on the wild side of life. This is no Father Christmas comfort faith. It also includes a system of belief that leads to relevant engagement in the world. Some of its key dimensions follow. I have taken them from the first and last books of the Bible.

Four Genesis portraits

Here are four quick snapshots from Genesis that help to shape the attitudes of those who attempt to follow the teaching of the Bible. None are about comfort or easy placebos, but rather each requires a strong commitment to life and the well-being of the world.

A good world

The opening chapter of the Bible affirms that God created a good world. Whatever happened subsequently, the intent behind creation was positive. It is also a purposeful world – one deliberately created by a God who planned to do a good thing. In itself, this is a key building block of a Christian world view. This is not an accidental planet without any inherent purpose. To the contrary, God's purpose in creating the world confers meaning upon it. It is a meaning that is linked to the motivation of the Creator, and it is one which provides direction to the creation when it is discovered. This naturally invites us to explore the reasons for creation, and the opening portrait of the Bible gives a sense that this purpose is to be discovered in intimate and ongoing relationship with the Creator.

After describing and affirming the goodness of the non-human creation in verses 1–25, Genesis 1 informs us that humans (both male and female) are created in the image of God (vv. 26–31) – a lofty status indeed. If their status is impressive, their task is daunting, for they are to represent God in the world. The account throbs with optimism and hope. God has created the world, but humanity must now grow and manage the world.

Building a world with a better name

The contours of their task as God's representatives find early expression when Adam is instructed to name the birds and the animals (Gen. 2:19–20). Don't be fooled by what may sound a simple task. Names in the Bible are very significant, for your name is a window to who you are. When Adam is instructed to name creation, he is essentially being told to humanize the world – or, as I have expressed it elsewhere, to build a world with a better name.[9] God watches as Adam does this. The sense is that God is deeply interested in the choices made, but does not interfere in them. The portrait is liberating. God has created the world, and people must now make it a special place – a place where everything belongs and has found its true name.

Those who want to dismiss Christianity as escapist or illusionary must grapple with this. This is not hiding for cover in some illusionary and gentle fairy tale; it is embracing responsibility for the well-being of the planet. If species disappear, it is because we have failed to preserve their name. If the world is not in harmony, it is because we have not helped it to find its true name.

The image also disallows toxic forms of faith which block the door to progress in the name of God. God made the world, but humanity must complete what God started. It is rather like a builder who constructs a house, but leaves it to the purchaser to make it a home. Both tasks are essential. Being made in the image of God is both an awesome privilege and a sobering responsibility. It thrusts us into active engagement with the world.

A fallen world

Part of the dignity of being made in the image of God is the ability to choose. While complete freedom of choice has never really existed (we are all shaped by our time and setting), we are responsible for significant areas of life and for the decisions we make. Even in paradise, there was the option to choose to rebel, and the biblical account tells the story of Adam and Eve's fall from grace, when they chose to disobey the Creator's instruction to refrain from eating the fruit from the tree of the knowledge of good and evil. This act is the Bible's explanation for the entry of sin and suffering into the world.

It is important to note what the Bible does and does not say about this fall from grace. Humans did not forfeit their standing as the only beings made in God's image. To the contrary, Genesis 9:6, written well after the fall, insists that we must not murder because the person we kill is made in the image of God. We are thus tarnished image bearers living in a world that is no longer as it should be, but still with the status of being God's representatives in the world.

It is significant that the Christian story takes evil seriously. As opposed to the naive optimism found in some forms of psychology (the Client Centred Therapy of Carl Rogers being a good example), where the essential goodness of each human being is accepted without question, the Bible has a healthy scepticism. People do indeed have the ability to do wonderful things. They also have the potential to do unspeakable harm. We need to factor both into our understanding of the world, and only this nuanced approach can leave us open to hope but realistic about the challenges to be faced.

Later passages in the Bible explore the problem of evil more deeply. They point ultimately to the cross of Jesus and to our need for grace and forgiveness . . . but let me not run ahead to material to be covered in Chapter 7.

Standing in the gap

Genesis 18:16–33 is the sobering account of angelic visitors to Abraham who, after completing their business with Abraham and Sarah, announce their intention of visiting the nearby city of Sodom to see if it is as wicked as has been reported. Abraham, fully aware that Sodom's atrocities have not been exaggerated, realizes that the inevitable outcome of the investigation will be the destruction of Sodom. In spite of the city's great evil, Abraham responds with concern and compassion. True, some of his relatives live in the city, but his distress over its likely plight seems to have a deeper foundation. He is worried that both good and evil people will be consumed, and is troubled that God's reputation for justice could be compromised, leading him to boldly ask God in verse 25, 'Will not the Judge of all the earth do right?'

An interesting scenario then unfolds. Abraham pleads for Sodom, asking initially that if fifty righteous people are found in the city, that God spare it for the sake of the fifty. God agrees. Abraham, recognizing that a target of fifty was ambitious, progressively negotiates the number down to ten. However, even ten proves excessive, and God removes the only four righteous people who can be found – Lot, his wife and two daughters, although Lot's wife is not to survive the ordeal. The city is then destroyed.

Sad though the story is, the implications behind it are impressive and challenging. Apparently a few righteous people in a town (as few as ten – the number of men required in later Judaism to form a synagogue in a town) can dramatically impact its welfare. It is a forerunner to Jesus' later teaching that Christians are the salt and the light of the world (Matt. 5:13–16). If Genesis 2:19–20 suggests that we should build a world with a better name, Genesis 18:16–33 suggests that we should stand in the gap for a struggling humanity, helping to turn its fortunes around by pointing them to the God who created and cares for them. Again, this is an adventurous and stretching call. It is not for the faint-hearted, nor is it for those who, too afraid of the pressures and sadness of life, wish to retreat into a fantasy world of their own creation. It is about being unafraid to enter the broken and struggling places of life, and being committed to making a difference in them.

A Revelation portrait: a new heaven and a new earth

Let's supplement the four quick snapshots from the opening book of the Bible with one from its closing book, found in Revelation 21:1–4. I mentioned it briefly in the previous chapter, noting that in toxic forms of faith, eschatology often becomes escapist. Equally, it can be accused of speaking of an illusionary state – a happy heavenly realm where we sing together for all of eternity, relieved that we are at last released from all the strains and stresses experienced during our earthly existence. If this is what the Bible teaches we can agree with Freud, because such a portrait is little more than a wishful longing to be released from the pressures of life.

However, Christian eschatology presents a far more challenging portrait of the future of the world. Those who enter the doorway to life opened by Jesus should not expect a future in some alternative universe or in a place called 'heaven'. According to John's vision, their destiny is the new earth – not an alternative earth, but an earth that is now as it was always intended to be. This validates God's initial creation of a good earth. Rather than this planet being abandoned as an unfortunate and failed experiment, it is to be renewed – which is what is meant by 'a new earth'. The categories are not radically different from the past. There will no doubt be work and other responsibilities to be fulfilled. The striking difference is that, to quote the cry raised in Revelation 21:3 (GNT), 'Now God's home is with people. He will live with them, and they shall be his people. God himself will be with them, and he will be their God.' God intends to live permanently on the earth made new.

Multiple implications spring from this portrait and beg to be unpacked. For our purposes, one is especially striking. If a renewed earth is our future destiny, current efforts to value this planet are well founded. It is the location for eternity. True, it will be a new earth, but the name 'earth' remains, and names in the Bible always get to the heart of things. The basic thinking and assumptions behind the creation of the earth are upheld. We in part equip ourselves for life on this renewed planet by taking our original creation mandate seriously. When we build a world with a better name, we are moving in step with God's plan to ultimately renew this planet.

This, then, is no dreaming for an alternative reality. It is about deep commitment to the world that is, and the world that could be if we accept our responsibility as those made in God's image, called to be responsible stewards of this planet.

What Does This Mean?

This chapter has not attempted to deny that religion can sometimes be a comforting illusion. Life can be extremely difficult, at times even cruel. At critical points in life we sense our vulnerability and it is only natural that we then long for a safer, kinder world. We might indeed project this longing onto a divine being who is supposed to provide what we long for. The mind is its own place and does sometimes lead us on unexpected paths, especially when we are under great stress. That we console ourselves with comforting but improbable stories at such times is natural enough.

What is more remarkable is not that religion is sometimes illusionary, but that so often it is not. We need to sit up and take notice when religion's role shifts from being a comforting placebo to a force that motivates mature and relevant engagement in the world. This is where the views of Freud and others are shown to be limited. It is easy to understand why we seek solace in religion, but less easy to understand why we allow it to challenge and stretch us to paths of sacrifice and service. Allport is right. For some it is because their religious orientation is deeply intrinsic – it is the essence of who they are. It is not an illusion. They are not running from life when they serve the God they worship and adore – this is their life, and they find it to be deeply and profoundly satisfying.

For others, religion legitimates the quest for truth. Starting from the deep conviction that a loving God has created the world, they refuse to settle for shallow responses, and actively strive to find answers to life's most perplexing questions. They long to build a world with a better name, and often find in the Christian metanarrative the images and symbols they need to constructively engage with the world. Such reactions are wholesome and good, and should be celebrated and applauded.

Yet a shadow side is never far from the surface. Life-serving faith can degenerate into toxic faith. We can clothe our longing for grandeur in religious jargon about call, purpose and prophecy. We can fail to differentiate between God's kingdom and our own, and convince ourselves that in protecting our personal comfort zone, we are furthering God's work. Tragically, we can allow religious prejudice to block us from seeing the good in others, and allow it to prevent us from spotting our common humanity. We can even use our faith as an excuse to exclude us from the quest for justice and humane progress. Horrible caricatures of faith are easy to find, and we may fall prey to them if we are not on our guard.

To avoid these traps, it helps if we orientate ourselves with our founding stories – the significant building blocks of the Christian metanarrative. These blocks persistently point us towards a life of engagement in God's world. They never justify a flight from reality.

They help us to understand the depths of human depravity, while also reminding us of the magnitude of our potential as image bearers of the God who made us. Although they alert us that this world is not all that there is, they also affirm the value of what is done on this planet – for a renewed earth will be the location of God's permanent dwelling with humanity.

When we truly listen to this story, we roll up our sleeves, say 'yes' to God and to life, and constructively and hopefully embrace the call to build a world with a better name.

In Conversation with Yvonne Kilpatrick

Yvonne Kilpatrick is a psychologist and works as a counsellor. She is involved in a church she considers to be life-affirming but has had many conversations with friends and clients who have experienced toxic faith.

As a psychologist, do you sometimes see people use faith to avoid facing the harder issues of life? If so, what alerts you to this?

Yes, I do sometimes see faith used as an anaesthetic and blindfold. We all want to avoid pain – whether it is physical, emotional or spiritual – and we use whatever is at hand, including our religious beliefs. When faith is used to avoid the pain or uncertainty that are pretty much a guaranteed part of being human, I'm alerted by pat answers, clichés and over-spiritualizing. Another sign is judgement of others, perhaps as a distorted way of bolstering self-worth and the correctness of a particular flavour of religion. Perhaps faith as self-protection is most visible when we are struggling to respond adequately to others' pain. We might say, 'I'll pray for you' and then leave them alone; or 'Everything happens for a reason', which has the same distancing effect. Faith can be a great source of hope and strength in hard times, but not when it is used to keep us from facing them or joining with others in facing theirs.

You've had contact with people who have been caught up in sects. Why do sects appeal to some people, and what damage do they cause?

Sects tend to appeal to people who are idealistic and have a low tolerance of ambiguity. They are often intelligent, well-adjusted people searching for meaning and at a turning point in life. In a sense they are not so much vulnerable people as they are people at a vulnerable stage who resonate with the absolutes, sense of community, purpose and idealism of the sect. For those growing up in a sect, their outlooks are shaped from the beginning to conform to the group and not to question authority. Because sects can envelop the person's whole life and identity, they are usually very difficult to leave. The damage caused is likely to be proportionate to the degree of control exercised over members and any abuse that has occurred. Ex-members report struggling with trust, self-confidence, alienation, anxiety, depression and trauma-related issues. We may be confident our church is not a sect, but we must always be careful that we don't use faith to control people. We cannot be preoccupied with appearances and behaviour at the expense of real relationships and real faith journeys.

Do you think genuine Christian faith promotes psychological well-being, and if so, why?

I absolutely do! As a psychologist who is known to be a Christian, I see a high proportion of Christian clients, which has made me wonder at times about the relationship between faith and mental health. In investigating the relevant literature in order to respond to this chapter, I was encouraged to find that most recent research indicates that religious beliefs are, in general, protective of mental health. For instance, they are positively associated with factors such as hope, optimism, self-esteem, purpose and belonging. Faith is also linked with lower rates of anxiety, suicide, psychosis, drug use and criminality, and with higher levels of marital stability and satisfaction. The Christian faith, in particular, promotes well-being in that God's love is unconditional and the faith is centred on relationship rather than a system. The unconditional love at the heart of a genuine Christian faith provides a foundation for a solid sense of worth and identity that can permeate every experience and relationship.

What do you see as being the conditions that contribute to toxic faith?

In terms of individual mental health, extrinsic religiousness is a major contributor to the development of toxic faith. In other words, when faith is used to achieve personal or social goals, such as power, status, self-justification, distraction and personal comfort, it is associated with poorer mental health. For example, higher levels of guilt, anxiety, depressive symptoms and prejudice have been linked to extrinsic religiousness.

Faith that is used in a toxic way towards others requires a system to support it as well as individuals willing to wield it. In my view, the conditions which favour that are total authority of leaders; a focus on 'doing' Christian things that is not balanced with the unquantifiable 'being' in relationship with God; and suspiciousness towards those who see faith differently. There is also a lack of questioning and struggling with complex issues together. In contrast, healthy faith does not have all the loose ends tied up neatly but it does have a confident core – a confidence in God's love for us all that fosters health, including mental health. As a psychologist, I find that incredibly energizing and it motivates me to find more and better ways to incorporate clients' faith experiences in therapy. I am grateful for your thought-provoking chapter and the opportunity to respond.

To Ponder and Discuss

1. What kind of faith do you have: extrinsic, intrinsic or questing? Why do you see yourself in this way?
2. What do you think of the statement 'What is remarkable is not that religion is sometimes illusionary, but that it so often is not'? Do you agree with the sentiment?

3. Are there people you know who have confused God's kingdom with their own?

4. Has your faith motivated you to roll up your sleeves, say 'yes' to God and to life, and to constructively and hopefully embrace the call to build a world with a better name? If not, what has it motivated you to do?

5

Hitchens: Faith as Poisonous

An Encouraging Story

I remember her well. I knew nothing about her when she started attending the church where I was pastor, but she struck me as one of those people for whom life has been difficult. Nothing tangible to prove that: she dressed fashionably, drove a new car and lived in the area – a very pleasant middle-class suburb. But people give other cues that all is not well.

Initially I dismissed it as her feeling a little unsettled in a new environment. It was clear that she didn't know much about the Christian faith, though she was familiar with the major themes and knew one or two of the older songs we sang. I wondered if she would attend for long, or if she would be one of the casualties of the church back door, slowly becoming less and less regular until she no longer came at all.

But the opposite occurred. She started attending almost everything. And as she did so, we got to know her story better. Nothing too dramatic about it. The fourth of five children, she felt overlooked when growing up. She was fairly philosophical about it. She had raised two children of her own and wondered how her mother had ever managed with five. She had been married. There had been a fair number of good years, but then, as she put it, 'He traded me in for a younger model. It happens. Men, you know . . .' She said it lightly enough, but beneath those words were a world of pain. 'You carry on. What else can you do?' Her children were grown, doing well actually, but now living in another city. 'You know what it's like. They have to find their own way.' I didn't ask, but I suspected that they didn't phone home very often.

A few months later we held a church camp. It was one of those hilarious and wonderful times when people, camp speaker and weather work harmoniously to provide a stunning forty-eight hours. At the end we gave people a chance to say what the weekend had meant to them. The regulars quickly got to their feet and affirmed the value of our time together. This had definitely been a time of spiritual growth for many – you could sense that the bonds between people had been woven together more tightly.

And then she got up. It was the first time she had spoken to the group as a whole, and I wondered how she would fare. She spoke with more than a little emotion. 'Thank you,' she said. 'I just want to say thank you. I'm 56 years old and this is the first time in my life that I have felt as though I belong. I think I now really do have a family, and I cannot begin to tell you what a difference that makes . . . oh, what a difference that makes!'

She later told us that she wasn't quite sure when it had happened, but at some point in the journey with us she had discovered that Jesus was real. 'It's not that I was opposed to it before. It just didn't seem to apply to me. But that's changed now – completely changed. I now know that I am never alone. Never alone . . .'

I could have selected a more spectacular story. In the course of my years as a pastor I have seen people released from drug and alcohol addiction, families restored, people who were thought to be incurably ill healed, and many, many lives turned around. But it is the ordinariness of this story that appeals to me. It happens so often. Churches are filled with people who have found in them a true home, a place to flourish.

It is why when I first read Christopher Hitchens' book *God Is Not Great: How Religion Poisons Everything*, I was genuinely perplexed. My own experience of faith, and of the Christian faith in particular, had been so different. Poisonous – the accusation seemed most excessive. I was surrounded by people who had found Christianity to be liberating and life-transforming. But as I read the book, and others of its ilk, I found myself reluctantly coming to the conclusion that religious faith – and the Christian faith must be included in this – can become toxic. It depends on whether we fall into some enticing traps, or note them and avoid them.

This chapter is not meant to be an exercise in negativity, but it will unpack some areas where we may unwittingly turn that which is most precious to us into a curse and a burden, both for ourselves and for others. Some revolve around unhelpful attitudes we can allow to develop; others are more systemic and touch on the potential for abuse when faith gains power in a society, and can influence societal direction.

First, let's re-familiarize ourselves with some of the common charges made against religion. In our opening chapter I suggested the following list of ten. In one way or another, religion is considered guilty of:

1. Religious warfare
2. Colonial exploitation
3. Racial bigotry
4. The subjugation of women
5. Homophobia
6. The abuse of the environment
7. Retarding the progress of science – especially medical science
8. Academic censorship
9. Intolerance of anything new
10. Sexual abuse, especially of children

I also referred to David Kinnaman and Gabe Lyons' study of the attitude of 16–29-year-old Americans towards Christianity.[1] They noted six recurring images of Christians, who were considered to be:

1. Hypocritical
2. Interested in 'saving' people rather than in relating to them
3. Anti-homosexual
4. Sheltered
5. Too political
6. Judgemental

I will select from these lists, grouping first a set of attitudes from them which we must work to avoid, and then following this with some traps to be avoided when we are in positions of influence and power.

Attitudes to Avoid

Perhaps the most common attitudinal risk is that of developing a 'them and us' mentality. Before our conversion to Christ, we probably saw ourselves as part of the great pool of humanity. To be sure, we had our preferences and idiosyncrasies, our fanatical support of the football team that persistently lost or our love of opera, but when push came to shove we saw ourselves as much the same as everyone else, needing to earn enough money to keep food on the table, and doing our best to stave off the inevitable day of our death.

That changed the day we said 'yes' to Jesus. Suddenly we were part of a group who saw themselves as called to make a difference in the world. That group had a mission to invite those who had not yet responded to Jesus to do so. We started to think in terms of those who were part of our group and those who were not. Perhaps we were urged from the pulpit to invite our 'unsaved' neighbours to certain church events which were seeker-friendly. It was probably suggested that at those events our friends might be persuaded to become one of us.

This is a genuinely difficult area. Conversion to Christ changes many things, and following his lead requires us to march to the beat of a different drummer.

I became acutely aware of this when the church where I was pastor some time back decided to adopt a mission slogan. We wanted something catchy which would help the congregation know what we were on about. After much discussion we decided we needed a statement that captured a sense of our own need for growth and change as well as our commitment to our area. After much discussion this morphed into the catchphrase we adopted: 'Reaching the lost; transforming the found.'

Initially we loved it, and it proved genuinely helpful – helpful for us, that is; not for our community. We could explain to those who attended the church the lens through which we evaluated all proposed church events. They needed to make a relevant difference in our area (reaching the lost) or to deepen our discipleship (transforming the found).

We were fully involved in our area – a great local church. One of our ministries was to new migrants, many of whom had limited English. Over a hundred attended the English classes which we ran. One of them was fascinated by the slogan. 'Are you saying I am lost?' he asked. 'I'm not lost. I know where I am.' And he roared with laughter. I tried to explain, but he would have none of it. Nor would our wider community. In one way and another they let us know they felt we were snubbing them or judging them, by suggesting that they were lost and we were found.

In time we came to our senses and adopted a new motto: 'Digging deeper, reaching wider.' It might still be in use.

The 'them–us' dilemma comes into even sharper focus when the church attempts to act as the moral watchdog of society. Again, this is a very difficult area. Following Jesus has ethical implications. It does impact our attitude to sex, pornography, our use of money and our attitude to the larger social issues of our time. When we speak about these convictions, those who have made different decisions often feel uncomfortable and as though we are judging them – which we often are. 'Are you really telling me that I shouldn't try before I buy and have no sex before marriage? Get a life!'

It is these kinds of scenarios that led the twenty-somethings of Kinnaman and Lyons' study to dismiss Christians as being interested in people only in order to save them rather than to relate to them, and as judgemental. We need to grapple with this deeply. In the end, attitudes are sensed rather than articulated. In other words, it is not really about what we say, but what people feel when they are in our presence. It is about our willingness to enter into two-way relationships. It is about our being prepared to be vulnerable, and not having every answer neatly packaged.

What about some of the other issues raised in the Kinnaman and Lyons study? Are Christians hypocrites? Do they, for example, extol the virtues of family life while their own homes are in tatters? Although some studies suggest that Christian marriages are more likely to end in divorce than those of people with no religious faith, more careful analysis of the data shows that this is only true when you include those whose faith is very nominal. When you restrict the label of a 'religious couple' to those who actively practise their faith and demonstrate this by regular church attendance and religious observance, divorce rates are significantly lower than for the general population. Actively practising Catholics have been shown to be 31 per cent less likely to divorce than those of no religion, and practising Protestants 35 per cent less likely; while if we widen the survey to include practising Jewish couples, there is an impressive 97 per cent lower likelihood of divorce.[2] So practising Christians do have some credibility here. Not that faith inoculates one from the difficulties of life, but it does seem that principles such as commitment and forgiveness do work in practice.

Why, then, is the accusation of hypocrisy so readily made? Perhaps people of faith need to remember the ambivalence with which those of no faith watch their behaviour. On the one hand, there is a measure of smug delight when things go wrong for the faithful: 'Told you so. They're no better than the rest of us. They just think they are.' Simultaneously, there is an enormous sense of disappointment: 'If they can't get it right, what hope is there for the rest of us?'

The failure of a person of faith feels like a double betrayal. Society is justifiably angry every time a child is molested, but that anger knows no limits when the perpetrator is a religious leader. After all, if you can't trust the church, who can you trust? In its own way, this is a backhanded compliment. People long for higher standards from the church. They expect it to be a beacon of love, hope and purity. When it is not, bitter disappointment overflows into shrill accusations of hypocrisy – 'You of all people!' is the despairing subscript. It is a serious thing to accept the call to follow Jesus the Christ, and those who answer it need to be realistic about the responsibility it places upon them.

Kinnaman and Lyons' study saw Christians accused of being sheltered. There might well be something in this, and it isn't necessarily negative. One of the reasons why the marriages of practising Christians are more likely to succeed is that they put boundaries in place and refuse to expose themselves to the seamier side of life. There is another side to this, though. While Christians are usually coy and cautious about that which might challenge their personal morality, better churches are ensuring that their members are fully informed on the social justice questions of our time. Many organize short-term mission exposure trips, where participants come face-to-face with extreme poverty and injustice. Those who cannot go in person are shown video clips and hear the reports of those who went. Lives and lifestyles are often changed as a result. There is nothing sheltered about this.

But let us not dismiss Kinnaman and Lyons' participants' concerns too quickly. Many churches run busy programmes, and they need to be staffed by volunteers to run effectively. The new convert to Christianity often finds that it is not just Sunday that is taken up by their new faith. The Wednesday night programme is suddenly a 'must attend', and then there is a task force meeting most Mondays, and the music team practices on Thursday . . . and so it goes on. It is not unusual for all discretionary time to be taken up by worthy church events. Friends from the pre-Christian era are not intentionally ignored, but there is simply no time for them. Understandably, they think they have lost their former friend to the sheltering cocoon of the church, and they feel the loss.

Again, answers to this dilemma can prove elusive, but a start is made when we clearly articulate the problem. The absence of Christians at the local pub, sports club or drama society runs contrary to Jesus' vision of his followers being salt and light to the world. At times, church leaders need to intentionally release their members from involvement in church activities so that they can have time to coach the under-11 soccer team or participate in a community clean-up of the local river. Jesus' model of engagement in the world was that of incarnation – being there. Each local church should evaluate the extent to which it helps its members to genuinely be there for the community. Perhaps we should boast less of growing attendance at church programmes, and more of increasing engagement in our setting. This is a sure way to defuse accusations of leading sheltered lives, and will give us a window on the world God loves so dearly.

What about the other two charges on Kinnaman and Lyons' list: that Christians are anti-homosexual and too political? At times the two seem related, as churches around the world have been at the forefront of opposition to gay marriage and have often been very astute in the way in which they have mobilized political opposition.

This is a genuinely complex issue. Christians have to grapple with questions of hermeneutics as they try to decide an appropriate way to make sense of biblical passages that refer to homosexual behaviour. What once seemed straightforward – namely, that the Bible opposed any such practice – is increasingly being challenged, and it is possible that many scholars will shift their stance on this in the coming years.[3] Time will tell.

In addition, many are genuinely uncertain as to what response will lead to the greater public good. Those who advocate for gay marriage are confident that gaining this legal right will reverse a significant injustice, and that the reversal of any injustice is ultimately always for the greater good. Those opposed are doubtful and fear that a raft of unanticipated and unintended consequences will follow. Sometimes these are linked to the adoptive rights of gay couples, but fears raised are not restricted to this.

While the average Christ-follower is unlikely to be able to significantly impact the direction of this debate, the power of attitudes expressed towards the LGBTI community should not be underestimated and is at the heart of the criticism expressed by those interviewed by Kinnaman and Lyons.

An insight from Anton Boisen (1876–1965), founder of the clinical pastoral education movement, can provide some direction here. After his hospitalization for mental illness, he realized how irrelevant and unhelpful had been the assistance he received. The pastoral support offered had seemed bookish and unrelated to the reality of who he was as a person and what he was going through. In the book which flowed from his experience, *The Exploration of the Inner World*, he urged that theological students study not only books but also 'the living human documents'.[4] His expression has become famous and it gets to the heart of what we so often fail to do. We often don't actually listen to the stories we are being told. People are too quickly categorized and placed into a theoretical or theological box. 'This person is gay but not in a gay sexual relationship and therefore our answer to them should be . . . This person is gay and in a sexual relationship, so now the answer must change to . . .'

I even know of some churches that have devised answer sheets for their staff so that they will know how to respond to the queries of gay people as to what they can or cannot do at the church. To see it listed as a series of answers to frequently asked questions is perturbing. It is deeply dehumanizing. Clearly the individual's story is being ignored.

By contrast, those who follow the Messiah will have open hearts, open minds and open lives as they interact with those they come into contact with. Deep listening must precede the provision of answers, and if it does not, our faith has served as a barrier preventing us from being open to the humanity of the other. This can only be classified as toxic.

Some will undoubtedly object that this is a dangerously subjective approach, and that it implies that there are no moral absolutes to which Christians can hold. They might say, 'We don't need to listen to the rationalization of an adulterous couple as to why their relationship is special and should not need to comply with the usual Christian prohibition of adultery. There is an objectivity to certain moral laws, and it is reckless to pretend otherwise.' This objection has merit and should not be glossed over. But what should not be overlooked is the depth of human pain caused by some struggles. Sexual identity is one such area. The announcement that someone is lesbian or gay in their sexual orientation is usually preceded by years of struggle and angst. Some never find the courage to name their identity. This is simply not in the same category as a casual sexual fling or of succumbing to some minor temptation. Far more is at stake, and those who have made this journey are owed the dignity of having their story listened to and respected.

Genuine openness to the people and communities in which we are incarnated will usually provide a life-serving path beyond the disappointed observations on Kinnaman and Lyons' list. Rather than retort defensively, with a 'That's so unfair, and I will show you why it is not true' response, we should view the list as a gift to us. There is indeed much truth in what is said. Avoiding these traps will not prove easy, and we will often fail. But a start is made when we face what we are up against. Each local church would do well to spend some time interrogating their practices in the light of each of the six accusations Kinnaman and Lyons cite.

Systemic Risks

While we started our exploration of poisonous faith at the level of individual attitudes, Hitchens' concerns are focused more on the societal impact of religious faith. The relationship of religion to war, colonization, racism, slowing the progress of science and other such areas must be explored if we are to highlight those attitudes likely to lead to life-serving practices, and others which will degenerate into the toxic.

There is a significant paradox to note and it is confusing and perplexing. There are so many wonderful societal advances that can be attributed to the active engagement of Christians in society and as a result of the church raising its voice to protect groups against one evil or another.

Did Christianity help to eliminate slavery from large parts of the world? Yes, and there is no doubt that William Wilberforce's strong Christian faith helped provide him with the courage and moral conviction to overcome the many obstacles he encountered as he headed the campaign that led to the Slavery Abolition Act of 1833, which outlawed slavery in most of the British Empire. That Wilberforce died just three days after the passage of this Act through Parliament was assured is especially poignant. Knowing his life's work was done, he could depart to his reward.

Yet we dare not overlook the fact that some of Wilberforce's staunchest opponents relentlessly quoted Bible passages at him, accusing him of ignoring what seemed to them to be the clear teaching of Scripture. While few today would pay attention to the hermeneutical approach adopted by these detractors, their objections were taken with the utmost seriousness in their day, and serve as a sobering reminder that the trite quoting of Bible verses can be deeply problematic.

What, then, are we to make of the accusations of Hitchens and others? Is religion poisonous? Is its inevitable outcome religious wars and the like?

At times the answer is undoubtedly 'yes'. It is difficult to pretend that the Crusades were unrelated to the Christian faith that inspired, motivated and seemed to justify those bloodthirsty campaigns. To try to sidestep responsibility for this is foolish. And lest we think that such atrocities are confined to a long-past era, it is challenging to realize that in the Rwandan Civil War (1990–4), Hutu preachers regularly cited King Saul's failure to heed God's instruction in 1 Samuel 15 to utterly destroy the Amalekites, including their children, infants and cattle, and warned that the Hutus would face a similar rejection by God if they failed to totally destroy their Tutsi neighbours. Their congregations were all too obedient. Philip Jenkins comments sadly and resignedly on this tragic misapplication of Scripture: 'The last Christian who will seek to exterminate another nation on the pretense of killing Amalekites has not yet been born.'[5]

In this Rwandan example, part of the problem was an unacceptable reading and interpretation of Scripture. In Chapter 10 I will unpack the thesis that we should read the Bible with the core conviction that the gospel liberates, and that any reading of Scripture that promotes or justifies oppression or injustice is unquestionably flawed. I will leave the rationale for this until then, but at this stage it is important to note that the Bible does contain troubling verses and that we need to come to terms with what Eric Seibert calls 'disturbing divine behavior'.[6] Unless we develop a robust hermeneutical approach, we can all too easily fall prey to using the Bible's more bloodthirsty passages to justify violence we would like to sanction and sanctify. There are far too many examples of this occurring for us to bury our heads in the sand, ostrich like, and pretend that it cannot happen.

Lest you wonder why I am citing examples of violence committed by Christians, I am well aware that there are many instances of violence committed by other religions – Islamic fundamentalism springing quickly to mind. However, I prefer to keep my critique to my own faith, without pretending that others are not complicit as well.

What about the accusation that religion retards scientific progress? It is true that most religions are instinctively conservative and wary of the new and untested. The myth of Pandora's box which, once opened, cannot again be made to contain all the evil released, is often the fearful image employed. When new projects are proposed, religious ethicists often rush to worst-case scenarios, thinking that the alarm generated will still the quest for alternatives. True, this assessment is a little harsh, but it is wise to note the extremely cautious note sounded by religious leaders in the wake of calls to reassess approaches to euthanasia, IVF, stem-cell research and the like. A default drive of 'no' fails to inspire a watching world, especially those who have a deep emotional stake in the outcome.

A major part of the issue is that religious convictions regularly come across as being non-negotiable. They are often seen as divinely mandated, and a claim that a principle has been God-ordained is seen by the faithful as trumping any alternative perspective. Yet Jesus was prepared to summarize the driving principles of the Christian faith into two broad principles: total love for God, and complete love for the neighbour. It is worth listening to what Scot McKnight appropriately calls 'the Jesus creed'.[7] Here is the account from Mark 12:28b–31: '"Of all the commandments, which is the most important?" "The most important one," answered Jesus, "is this: 'Hear O Israel, the Lord our God, the Lord is one. Love the Lord your God with all your heart and with all your soul and with all your mind and with all your strength.' The second is this: 'Love your neighbour as yourself.' There is no commandment greater than these."'

All ethical construction should build outwards from these two underpinning principles. What we view as non-negotiable is sometimes a construct many layers above these principles. They were usually arrived at by appropriately applying these standards in a particular time and setting. And they worked for that season. The problem comes when we allow the conclusions of a previous era to fossilize and to prevent debate in the current era. We are better advised to go back to first principles. Given the resources and insights of our time, what does love for God mean in our own day? And what does love for the neighbour mean? Each generation and culture must ask these questions afresh. The conclusions of a previous era should be noted with respect, but we should not assume in advance that they must be slavishly embraced. If we do, we doom our faith to be an unhelpful brake on valid progress, and we relegate ourselves to the role of naysayers, forever dismissing the concerns of a society which longs for a more hopeful tomorrow.

Regaining the Right to Be Prophetic

In its better eras, the church has played a prophetic role in society. It is never comfortable to be a prophet, for invariably there are evils and power structures to be challenged. They rarely respond meekly to confrontation, and the ensuing conflict can be harrowing.

I have already noted that I grew up in apartheid South Africa. I observed first-hand the church at its finest and at its worst. Too often it was complicit in the evils of that time, but equally, it sometimes soared to meet the challenges of the era. Some of the prophetic voices were strong and penetrating, their names now well known. We should be forever grateful for the likes of Albert Lutuli, Albetina Sisulu (you strike a woman, you strike a rock), Desmond Tutu, Beyers Naudé, David Bosch, and a host of others. While they now bask in their status as moral giants, their road was fraught with difficulty and persecution. Ostracism, imprisonment and state sanction were often their lot – but this is sometimes par for the course for genuine prophets.

Sadly, in more recent days, it seems that the church has lost the right to be prophetic. It is reeling from too many accusations of sexual abuse. Its financial integrity is questioned. More fundamentally, it is perceived to act only in its own interests, and not on behalf of the flock it is called to shepherd, let alone the interests of the broader society in which it is located. It seems more concerned about its institutional well-being than its mission and call.

These are strong allegations, but they are made with increasing ferocity by those watching from the outside. Some never wanted the church to succeed and are rather pleased at the outcome. But for many there is a deep sense of disappointment and sadness. If the church has lost the right to be prophetic, who will step into the gaping hole left behind? Where is the moral centre of our society?

I will close this chapter with a simple thesis: regaining the right to a prophetic voice in society is one of the most important tasks facing the church. As a watching world often dismisses religious faith as poisoning everything, we need to repent of our failure to serve our time well. Rather than trying to safeguard our cherished traditions, we should be willing to embark on a risky venture of obedience. The model should be built on the incarnation of Jesus. We should ask ourselves again and again, 'Are we present in the city for our own good, or for the good of the city?' And we should be unafraid to ask what it will mean to heed the call of the Jesus creed. Having a clear view of what it means to love God and to love the neighbour is the non-negotiable minimum if we are to regain the right to have a prophetic voice. And we should not forget that our neighbours include those who are not easily within our line of vision – the marginalized, the poor, and those from countries where every window on the world seems to be closed. If we do not act on their behalf, who will?

In Conversation with Deborah Hurn

Deborah Hurn is a research student at Vose Seminary. Some years ago she was expelled from her church. Here are some of her reflections on that time.

Deb, you had a painful split from your church some years ago. What was that about?

All my family were lifelong active members of a high-commitment fundamentalist lay sect in which women could not preach, read, pray aloud or serve as elders. In 2006–7 I changed my mind about the role of women and created a website with a collection of original articles that addressed the issue biblically. I did not otherwise propagate my views in our church, and we made every effort to remain as inoffensive and dependable as before. However, the elders removed my husband and adult sons from their speaking and leading offices (my husband had been secretary of our church for fifteen years and a Bible teacher all his adult life; our sons were involved in youth ministry), intensively presented only one view to affiliated churches in the city, and banned members from speaking to us. Using an unrelated constitutional clause regarding 'submission to the majority' they created a 'Catch 22' style survey of members' views on the silence of women. On the basis of the resulting majority, they demanded I remove my articles from the website or be excommunicated ('disfellowshipped'). I refused to do so and in due course received a letter of disfellowship. But within four days, because of my husband's extreme distress, I removed the articles, and the action was reversed.

What did you learn through the process?

Reform has ever been a bloody affair . . . for the reformers – as seen in the Old Testament prophets, the crucifixion of Christ and the history of the church. We learned that the 'immune system' of authoritarian groups operates similarly in every era. Those in power persecute 'heretics' to the full extent of secular law: that is to say, whether contemporary society allows murder, torture, eviction, demotion or only shunning, the institution will apply the maximum permissible force to eliminate threats. We also learned how the 'ordinary people' in a community would rather amputate valuable members and services than disturb the status quo. On the positive side (and there are many positives) the dislocation from community brought us much free time, the release from expectations and duty, and an unexpected commonality with rejected and lapsed ex-members who were so very understanding and accepting! As a direct result of the confusion and doubt I experienced in exile, I started formal theological studies, and have been delighted to discover the wider world of Christian thought and fellowship.

What still hurts when you think back to that time?

Until our own crisis of dissent, we had not fully realized how friendships in our sect were conditional upon compliance with a rigid creed and tradition, such that anyone who challenged or failed expectations would be eliminated. The process and outcome was deeply traumatic for us and our children, and the loss of community and identity continues to disrupt and divide our extended family years later. We were shocked and hurt that trusted friends allowed and even participated in our persecution. These were people we had known all our lives, sharing every social and spiritual experience and raising our children together. The long-term effect on our three married children continues to play out – they are now atheists, expressing varying degrees of blame towards us for having raised them within a religious community. Our two pre-teenagers, who also lost their friends and connections, experienced depression and dislocation and are now almost unchurched.

What do you think are some warning signals that a local church might be turning toxic?

In our case, the church tradition was already toxic because its foundational principles were dogma, uniformity and exclusivity. Controlling behaviour and stagnant numbers were put down to 'human nature' or 'the last days' and not to flawed theology. Likewise, dissent or under-commitment was seen as individual, rather than institutional, weakness, and indeed this is how my feminist 'rebellion' was interpreted – as spiritual failure. As long as we were accepted and relatively empowered within the community, we could not see how toxic it was. I have since had time to analyse the negative effects of the practices of total doctrinal conformity, separation from 'the world' and closed membership, and would list these among the most toxic elements for any church. All three are in fact opposed to Jesus' message and practice. He made no comment on many beliefs of the day, lived within society at all levels, and accepted and ministered to anyone.

What do you think are signs that a local church is a genuine centre of life and hope?

I must confess I am doubtful whether 'extractional' church models can operate as 'centres of life and hope'. I have moved to the view that our real lives in Christ are outside the church in our everyday relationships with family, friends and contacts – who may be of any faith or none. In a post-Christian society, I would prefer churches to operate as spiritual 'services' rather than as communities. Perhaps we need to move from the 'club' model of church to one where Christ is dispersed into the world through each of our unique and random 'social footprints' – we are not supposed to know all the same people! I love to go to church to worship, to be taught, comforted and inspired (I left our former sect), but I will avoid sourcing all my social needs within one network, or placing my spiritual welfare at the mercy of an institution, no matter how benign it may appear. I can see how church may provide community for the lonely, but I well know how if things go wrong, people who have come to depend on a church population for social support may lose not just a few contacts but all of them! A generous and tolerant outlook always offers more 'life and hope' than an agenda of conversion and conformity.

To Ponder and Discuss

1. How do you manage to juggle wanting people to come to faith in Jesus and not developing a 'them and us' mentality? Is this something that should concern us?

2. What do you think Anton Boisen meant when he suggested we study not only books but also 'the living human documents'? What implications might this have in practice?

3. Reflect on Philip Jenkins' comment that 'The last Christian who will seek to exterminate another nation on the pretense of killing Amalekites has not yet been born'. Is there anything we can do to reduce the likelihood that Jenkins is right?

4. Do you agree that the church's default drive is to say 'no' to the new and the innovative? How do we evaluate change, and how do we differentiate between that which violates fundamental Christian principles and that which is simply now possible due to our expanding knowledge base?

5. Do you agree that the church needs to regain the right to be prophetic? What might this mean in practice?

6

And What About . . . ? Some Other Temptations

A Worrying Story

She had asked to see me and was clearly very distraught. I had met her once or twice at combined church events but didn't really know her. As she entered my office, she immediately burst out, 'Kicked out. Told never to return. I've served there for twenty-two years. I can't believe it.' And then she dissolved into tears.

The story slowly came out, piece by piece. She had been concerned about the direction her church had been travelling. She felt that in their drive to professionalize, they were overlooking the needs of ordinary folk. Musicians now had to audition to serve on the worship team, and one of the guitarists, who had been part of the church band for over a decade, had been told he had failed to meet the required standard.

'Dumped. Just like that. No longer needed. Surplus to requirements. Well, I knew how much that had hurt him,' she explained. 'So I objected. I was told that if we were to reach our area, we had to improve our musical standards. He wasn't good enough, and at 47, he was unlikely to get much better, so the pastor said. I said I wasn't happy, and he replied that I needed to decide if I was on or off the bus. "What bus is that?" I asked. And he said I knew what he meant. If I didn't like where the church was going, there were plenty of others, and I could take my pick from any of them. I was stunned. This was the church I was married at. I've helped in the children's ministry for years. I've been part of every fundraising drive, and we've actually denied ourselves some fancy holidays so that we could contribute more generously to the church's needs . . . to his salary, actually. And he was making it clear that he couldn't care if I was there or not.'

I could see where the conversation was going. It was not the first of its kind that I had heard. 'So what happened next?' I asked.

'I've got to be honest,' she replied. 'I'm not the sort of person who backs away from a challenge. So I asked a few other people what they felt about what was happening. Lots and lots of unhappiness out there. The changes were supposed to help us grow, but actually we were getting smaller by the week. Perhaps that sounds like I was getting a gossip chain going, but believe it or not, I was trying to be helpful. I love that church, and have poured my life into it. I hate to see it going backwards.'

I waited for her to carry on. I could see that she found the next part difficult to say.

'And then I get this message. The pastor wants to see me. I go along, not sure what it's about, and when I get there he opens the Bible and reads from Psalm 105:15. Something about touching the Lord's anointed and doing his prophets harm. He said that was what I had done – that I was damaging the reputation of the Lord's anointed, and that I must therefore go. "Go?" I asked him. "Yes, you and your family," he replied. "You are unwelcome here. Don't ever come back." I thought he was joking. Just stared at him. Stunned. "That's all," he said. "Goodbye." And that's it,' she said. 'Kicked out. Told never to return. The kids can't understand it. Some of their best friends are in that place.'

And she wept some more . . .

Most churches are happy places, but sometimes things go wrong, and when they do, the emotional toll can be very high. The repercussions can continue for decades. This chapter is primarily about the triggers that can spark waves of toxicity in the local church. More positively, it explores ways to actualize Jesus' optimistic claim that those who watch us will know that we are Christians by the love that we demonstrate towards each other (John 13:35).

We will look at leadership traps to be avoided, the danger of putting the good of the institution above that of the individuals that make it up, the risk of adopting programmes that are likely to lead to burnout, and some of the muddled thinking that sometimes leads to problems.

Leadership Traps

There are three key 'S' requirements of those who would like to lead in a manner consistent with biblical principles:[1] leaders must be servants, shepherds and stewards. Better leaders might also manage another two 'S' words and serve as sages and seers, but the first three are non-negotiable, although they are often forgotten.

Speaking to his disciples after an unseemly squabble over who would be granted the seats closest to Jesus in the afterlife, Jesus instructs them: 'You know that the rulers of the Gentiles lord it over them, and their high officials exercise authority over them. Not so with you. Instead, whoever wants to be great among you must be your servant, and whoever wants to be first must be your slave – just as the Son of Man did not come to be served, but to serve, and to give his life as a ransom for many.'

These words from Matthew 20:25–28 are worth memorizing. They are counterintuitive. Instinctively we long for leadership as a means to gain importance, influence, perks and privileges. Jesus will have none of it. Leadership is about service, and about what happens to the people we are called to serve.

The term 'servant leadership' is often attached to biblical models of leadership.[2] The paradoxical linking of these two terms is one of the key features of most of the writing on leadership that flows from Christian authors. For example, Robert Greenleaf, in his book *Servant Leadership*, argues that leadership is 'bestowed' upon a person who is 'by nature a servant'. When trying to find a leader, the first thing to explore is the servant nature of the candidate, as this cannot be taken away. It represents the real person (one who desires to serve).

Leadership then becomes the way in which the person serves – and it is given if this is something the person is able to do well.[3] If the person is not able to serve via leadership, they will still serve the group but they will find other ways in which to do so. Indeed, most often a person is appointed to leadership after helpfully serving in a number of other capacities first. It is probably this sequence that Paul has in mind when he instructs Timothy to 'Never be in a hurry about appointing a church leader' (1 Tim. 5:22, NLT). We should first see what abilities a person has, and also be confident that giftedness is backed by an appropriate disposition and lifestyle.

The Bible is very affirming about the value of leadership and is clear that the desire to serve via the gift of leadership is honourable. In 1 Timothy 3:1 Paul says simply, 'To aspire to leadership is an honourable ambition' (NEB). It is honourable because it is about the desire to serve others and to help others and their groups become more than they would otherwise be.

Well, that's the theory at any rate! In reality, there is often a shadow side to the quest to lead.

Those who lead hold power, as leadership is about influence and being able to play a significant role in determining direction, staff appointments, the use of finance, and so on. The abuse of power can be a subtle temptation. In addition, leaders are sometimes considered to be a little larger than life. The praise and flattery of followers can lead to arrogance, pride and self-righteousness. Some people become leaders because they feel unsuccessful unless they lead. They can become addicted to the adrenaline rush that accompanies being able to set direction and the admiration that follows those who lead effectively. The journey from leading for the good of the group to leading for the sake of one's own ego can be short, and is sometimes embarked upon subtly. Some leaders are driven to lead and feel incomplete if they do not have others in tow, and will sometimes act irresponsibly to ensure that this situation remains.

We often make the mistake of looking for charismatic and confident leaders, but are sometimes better served by quiet leaders who come to their task a little reluctantly. These more hesitant leaders are usually conscious of the responsibility of helping to set the direction for a group of people or for an organization. They are willing to set aside their leadership if the interests of the group would be better served by another – especially if it is clear that this would be true over the longer term, and not just for a specific project or task. Not that charismatic leaders cannot also be effective servants; it is more that we are sometimes so dazzled by a potential leader's charisma that we fail to ask the more probing questions, and later lament the oversight.

The other two key 'S' words of leadership are also important.

Leaders are called to shepherd those who follow their lead. This refers to the nurture that good leadership provides. In larger groups, it may not be possible for the leader to provide this personally, but they will make sure that there are others who do. After all, good leadership is not about doing everything yourself, but about ensuring that all bases are covered.

When we are in nurturing church communities we surprise ourselves. Instead of running from our fears, we face them. At times we are helped to overcome them. We become a little more than we otherwise would have been. We are stretched without snapping, and the gentle flame of optimism starts to burn in our hearts. Instead of searching for reasons to say 'no', we happily find ways to say 'yes'. This is church as it is meant to be. And it isn't all leader-dependent. We bring the best out of each other . . . and it takes everyone to be part of this, as we create communities of encouragement, transparency and relevance. It's the kind of community described in Acts 2:42–47 and 4:32–35. The result was a church that grew rapidly, as people saw that the God talk was matched by generous and open-hearted lifestyles.

The third 'S' highlights the leader's need to be a steward. Although Christian leaders often struggle with resources that seem inadequate, they don't forget that they have often been provided by the generosity of others, sometimes at fair personal cost. They are also conscious that ultimately all resources come from God. They are therefore anxious to ensure that they are used effectively.

It can be difficult to be both a good shepherd and a responsible steward, but biblical leaders have to live with the tension inherent in these two requirements. Stewardship is about accountability – how well we use our time, finances and ability. It sometimes means challenging people, and questioning if they are acting wisely. While this is bread and butter stuff in standard employment relationships, in church life, where the pastoral leader is usually dealing with volunteers, it can be a lot more complex. What are we to do when a ministry leader performs a task poorly – or, to remember the incident that sparked our opening story, a musician is deemed not up to scratch?

It helps to differentiate between short- and long-term outcomes. A sympathetic but unchallenging pastoral conversation that avoids asking hard questions might be pleasant in the short term, but in the longer term might do the person a significant disservice in that it might reinforce unhelpful patterns of behaviour. Sometimes we need to love enough to challenge.

We can express it in terms of speaking the truth into situations. Biblically speaking, truth is only validly spoken when, first, it is actually the truth that we speak; second, we speak it in love (Eph. 4:15) – and therefore we should desist from telling 'home truths' to those we resent and dislike; and, third, it is spoken at the right time ('how good is a timely word!' Prov. 15:23). It is wise to refrain from speaking until we are sure that these three are in harmony – in other words, it is the truth, I really care for this person, and this seems to be a good time in their life to face a challenge. If we avoid this responsibility, we are neither good shepherds nor good stewards.

In addition to the three 'S' words – servant, shepherd and steward – the very best leaders also manage the other two.

They are sages whose wisdom not only guides the group they lead, but is also treasured by the individuals in the group. And they might also be seers, people able to sense not just the opportunities in the present moment but also the contours of the future. They therefore help their group not only to move, but to move in a direction that positions them to make a relevant contribution in the future.

All this is good leadership. It is important that we have a clear picture of what it should be. But we must not be unrealistic. The reality is that most groups are led by more ordinary leaders who on their better days might approach some of these qualities, but on others will fall well short. We should not be unduly harsh on those who are doing their best but not always fully succeeding. To the contrary, we should rally around them, helping to make up for their deficits. It is helpful to think of leaderships (plural) rather than leadership (singular); often, when we help support our pastoral leader we are exercising our own form of leadership.

While making allowances for the normal shortcomings of ordinary people, we should be aware that some leadership deficits fall outside this range and need to be challenged as being toxic. The sad opening example was one of an insecure leader lashing out at perfectly reasonable questions which were asked about some decisions made. When leaders view themselves as being above question, we are wise to switch on a red light of concern.

Here is a list of some common signs that leadership is going astray. When we spot them, and certainly if more than two or three are present, we need to think of ways to intervene. This list of ten is suggestive rather than definitive, and you can probably add to it – perhaps from your own experience:

1. When the leader demands unquestioning loyalty
2. When non-compliant followers are humiliated
3. When everyone but the leader is to blame whenever anything goes wrong
4. When looking good is more important than being good
5. When those who are uncertain of the validity of a decision are viewed as expendable, unless they back it
6. When the leader is the main beneficiary of the path advocated
7. When we are encouraged to think of an 'in' group and an 'out' group
8. When the past is ridiculed
9. When there is a climate of fear
10. When the truth, financial results or people are manipulated

In broad summary, toxic leaders abuse the leader–follower relationship. It is not just that they leave their group worse off than when they found it; the toll exacted on those who follow their lead is high and usually personal.

Let me say it again: it is not fair to expect every local church to have a high-calibre leader who stands well above critique. But we can expect that certain minimal standards will not be breeched. These standards often have more to do with personal integrity than competence; for a team of followers can usually compensate for gaps in competence, but a lack of integrity is always devastating.

Forgetting That People Matter

Because the church is such a worthy institution, it is easy to assume that its well-being trumps all other concerns. We quickly concur with a mindset that places its interests above others. There are more than enough dramatic examples to support our stance. The history of the church is full of inspiring stories of those who have died for the faith, and as the second-century church father Tertullian perceptively noted, 'the blood of the martyrs is the seed of the church'.[4] The willing sacrifice of martyrs, rather than stifling and suppressing the church, has most commonly led to its rapid growth, vindicating the value of sacrifice. It is hard to argue that this is not noble and good, and it sounds improper and insulting to those who have made such enormous sacrifices to even question the validity of such a stance.

It is, however, possible to misapply the insights of history and to conclude that every cost incurred for the church must be justified. We can assume that it is appropriate to require total loyalty to institutional well-being rather than the well-being of the individual. When we adopt this position, it is a small step to viewing church staff as pawns and volunteers as fair game. We can imagine that, provided we motivate people adequately, charging any emotional or fiscal price tag is acceptable. But it is not.

We must always remember that people matter. The Bible's opening portrait of humans depicts them as beings made in the image of God and therefore having a dignity that has been conferred upon them from the outside – a divinely given dignity. To treat them as minor pieces in a chess game of our own making is an outrageous violation of this dignity. People matter, and if we embark upon programmes which happily use then discard those who make it possible for them to take place, we are complicit in adopting a mercenary approach for some supposedly greater good.

The Bible's portrait of the creation of Adam is moving. He is made from the dust of the earth which is then animated by the breath of God (Gen. 2:7). What does it mean to be human? It is to be dust and breath. The first speaks of our frailty and vulnerability, the second of our grandeur. We might be the dust of the earth, but we are also the breath of God. Yet to forget that we are first the dust of the earth is to risk forgetting our weakness. We might adopt approaches that extol a greater price than we should ask.

An example may help here.

He had been a most effective youth pastor. He was strongly relational, and greatly loved by the youth. Their group had more than trebled with his shepherding care, and was now one of the largest in the area. True, he was a little absent-minded, and his organizational skills were less than impressive. The church board wondered if he was the right person to lead it into the future, but decided to put their concerns on hold while everything was going so well.

With many of the youth group in their final year of schooling and about to write the dreaded exams that accompanied that stage, he decided to hold a special service for them to which parents and relatives would also be invited. It was a good idea and strongly supported by the community, who turned up for the service in large numbers. Sadly, one of those who didn't arrive was the youth pastor himself. He really was absent-minded, and in his diary had recorded another date for the event. When it occurred, he was on a silent retreat day and couldn't be reached. Without his presence to co-ordinate the event, chaos ensued. The church board was both embarrassed and angry. They fired him instantly, explaining to the youth and congregation that they were sure they would be able to find someone who was better organized and who could help the youth group to grow to the next stage.

The church board was right. A replacement for the previous youth pastor was quickly found and in a short time, the youth group was growing strongly. Within a year, they were double their previous size, and the previous youth pastor was all but forgotten.

His life, however, was taking a very different turn. He couldn't believe that he had been summarily dismissed because he had muddled the date of his spiritual retreat with the youth pre-exam service. The group had grown so strongly during his tenure. He had so often gone out on a limb for the youth to help them out when they had got something wrong – why was no one willing to do the same for him? Unemployed, and brooding on these questions, he lapsed into a deeper and deeper depression. Six months later his wife announced he was no longer the cheerful, light-hearted person she had married, and she left. The divorce went through a little later. It was years before his life found some equilibrium again.

The church had flourished, but his life had collapsed.

It's a true story, and when I get groups to discuss it, they point out that there were a range of alternative options that the church board could have adopted. And they are right. But the truth is that they didn't explore those options – and the church flourished. I suspect that if you were to ask any member of the board about the incident they would reply, 'Yes, sad, wasn't it? But leaders have to make tough calls and it was obviously the right one. Look how the group flourished after we made that decision.' It is unlikely that any sense of angst would accompany the answer.

We can too easily assume that the well-being of the church is the only thing that really matters. But people also matter, and the impact of decisions on their lives must be taken just as seriously. This is true not only in employment decisions, but also when we embark upon seasons of change. It is not wrong to opt for change, but it is important that we carefully consider the unintended consequences that flow from change. In his work *Pyramids of Sacrifice*, sociologist Peter Berger notes how often groups promise a utopian future if an advocated change is adopted, but laments that they usually fail to adequately consider the cost of the proposed change.[5] He suggests that before any change is adopted we carefully do what he calls a calculus of meaning and offset it with the calculus of pain that the change is likely to cause. Before implementing change, we must be convinced that the calculus of meaning significantly outweighs the calculus of pain. He cautions that in doing this calculation, most groups greatly exaggerate the likely benefits of change, and significantly underestimate the costs.

This might sound reactionary and as though change should usually be resisted. Anyone who knows me will laugh and say, 'That doesn't sound like you at all!' And they are right. The church in the Western world is at a critical stage in its history and its fortunes will not reverse if it fights against change. But even as we forge a new path forward, we must ask how we can lessen the pain for those who find meaning and purpose in the present structures. There are many ways in which we can move towards the future. Blocking our ears to the pain of those impacted by difficult decisions is not one of those ways. The church matters – but so do people, and we must never forget this.

Cultivating Burnout

Peter Scazzero, in his book *Emotionally Healthy Spirituality*, warns of the danger of living without limits.[6] Because Christians are so often keen to serve others, they feel they have never quite done enough. There is always another need to meet, and sometimes we keep driving ourselves on to try to help. At other times we run away, but the sense of guilt that results from this is very discouraging. We know we are called to love others, but forget that self-love should also be included in this call.

St Ignatius of Loyola (1491–1556) recorded an inspiring but rather frightening prayer:

Lord, teach me to be generous.
Teach me to serve you as you deserve;

> to give and not to count the cost,
> to fight and not to heed the wounds,
> to toil and not to seek for rest,
> to labour and not to ask for reward,
> save that of knowing that I do your will.[7]

The prayer is undoubtedly beautiful. It is also emotionally dangerous, the glorification of a life without limits and a sure recipe for burnout unless many safeguards are in place.

David Bebbington, in his historical account of the rise of evangelicalism, notes that as a result of the stress on conversion and personal piety that arose from the Methodist revivals in the early nineteenth century, activism became a feature of those who had embraced this new-found version of faith.[8] People needed to be converted, and Christ-followers would do whatever it took to make that happen. Bebbington notes the change in the role of the average pastor at that time, and claims that before the revivals the average Anglican minister lived a life of relative ease, conducting services when required, but in many ways enjoying a lifestyle much the same as that of a country squire. This all changed with the advent of evangelicalism, and Bebbington records that the average Methodist minister was expected to work a ninety-hour week. The result was that many clergy burnt out, their needs being met by the establishment of the 'worn-out Methodist Ministers fund'. Once they had recovered, they could return to their ninety-hour week, before burning out again and seeking the fund's assistance yet again. No one seemed to think that the underlying model was toxic. The cause was so worthy that any price was justified, and there were always more unsaved people to be reached.

Burnout is one of the significant problems of our age, and religious burnout is one of its especially sad manifestations.

Christina Maslach, in her seminal work on burnout, suggests that it finds expression in three key areas: emotional exhaustion, detachment and a sense of lack of achievement.[9] While it can result from working too hard and too long, it is often related to overexposure to the needs and suffering of others. Compassion fatigue sets in, leaving those in the helping professions especially vulnerable to its consequences.

Identifying the risk of burnout is a helpful start to reducing the risk of falling prey to it. There are other tangible steps that can and should be taken.

Starting with a portrait of an ideal work setting is helpful. In their article 'Creating the Best Workplace on Earth', Goffee and Jones identify six virtuous organizational practices. While they acknowledge that 'the company of your dreams remains largely aspirational', they suggest that this dream company would:

1. Let people be themselves
2. Unleash the flow of information
3. Magnify people's strengths
4. Stand for more than shareholder value
5. Show how the daily work makes sense
6. Have rules people can believe in[10]

In other words, an ideal work setting is one where we can be ourselves, where we know what is actually going on, where our strengths are highlighted and developed, where our employer stands for something meaningful, where our daily work is fulfilling and where mindless rules don't exist.

Achieving this doesn't have to be that hard, and those who work in a church context, be it as a volunteer, or as a paid employee or member of the clergy, shouldn't consider it out of reach. After all, God does want to use our particular strengths, we are called to transparency and openness, we should bring the best out of each other, we certainly stand for something valuable and engage in daily work that is purposeful, and all this takes place against a deep conviction that grace is the reason our community has come together, so bondage to mindless rules or shallow legalism should never be an issue.

So why is burnout so often a problem in a church context?

Sometimes it is because it is hard to say 'no' in a church setting without feeling guilty. We also feel forced to please people, and often disguise what we really feel about something for fear of hurting or offending someone. We work with limited resources, and it seems as though there are never enough people or enough money to do what is required. No matter how well last Sunday went, another is just around the corner, and you are only as good as your last sermon (or youth programme, or choir performance, or whatever). The need around us never ends, and we are conscious of the ache that remains in so many hearts, in spite of our best efforts to help people come to terms with past losses and failures. There is no magic wand to make it all better, even though prayer does lighten the load for many. And then there is the pull of too many preferences and squabbling groups. Select upbeat music, and you please some but offend others. Move in a traditional direction, and you delight some but dismay others. It is impossible to please everyone, and at times it feels as though we please no one. Results are also difficult to determine. Point to the growing size of the congregation, and some will claim that it's because you are bowing to popular pressure and are selling out on the demands of the gospel. Try to justify a decline in size, and you'll be informed that you are running away from the obvious. The 'ministry is tough' list can go on and on.

Following his own experience of burnout, Carey Nieuwhof has helpfully blogged about nine signs that might indicate that you are burning out in leadership. It is probably useful to end our discussion on this topic by noting the signs, while adding the obvious: if this is you, it is time to seek help.

1. Your motivation has faded.
2. Your main emotion is numbness and you no longer feel the highs or lows.
3. People drain you.
4. Little things make you disproportionately angry.
5. You are becoming cynical.
6. Your productivity is dropping.

7. You are self-medicating.
8. You don't laugh any more.
9. Sleep and time off no longer refuel you.[11]

Muddled Thinking

We have looked at the risks of toxic leadership, or putting the church as an institution ahead of the needs of the people who make it up, and of the danger of burnout in ministry. There are many other traps that can trip us and turn what should be life-serving into that which is destructive and damaging. I conclude this chapter by noting a few risks that I put into the category of 'muddled thinking'. When we stand back from the situation, we spot what was going on, but when we are in the thick of it, it is not always so easy to see. Here are some examples.

There is the risk of being 'too kind' to require accountability. Church board members are sometimes conscious that those in ministry have arrived in their position as a result of significant sacrifice, and that they have turned down more promising job prospects to serve the local church. They feel that they should be grateful for whatever is offered, and sometimes don't interrogate the practices and decisions of the pastoral staff in the same way as they would employees of their own company. In the longer term, this is deeply demotivating. It can come across as our not seeming to care, or as though we think that the work of ministry doesn't really matter and that anything goes. Fairness and reasonableness are far safer guides than hiding from difficult situations. If someone seems to be underperforming, we should explore why. If an action promised at the last church board meeting has not taken place, we shouldn't act as though the pledge was not made. Conversations that prove difficult in the short term are often liberating in the longer term, and we mustn't run away from them because we are in a Christian setting.

We can also forget that a need is not a call. Church leaders sometimes imply that a vacancy in the leadership of the children's programme is a clear sign that someone has not obeyed God's call to serve. Those with tender consciences are easy prey and can be fooled into thinking that a need must be a call. But every vacancy does not have our name written alongside it, and we must refuse to be pressurized into thinking that it does.

Perhaps the most common pitfall is to assume that it all depends upon us. God does indeed wish to use us and does have a plan for our lives. The outworking of this plan is not necessarily the conversion of our neighbourhood or the transformation of our society. Sometimes our part is to simply be there, doing what we can while acutely aware of what we can't. We are all dependent on the grace and mercy of God. We are all created from the dust of the earth and by the breath of God. Our frailty is never far from us, but nor is our God-given dignity. That dignity is not related to our frenetic efforts to please God. It is a dignity freely conferred by our Creator and Redeemer. We must bask in the delight of being God's children. This is the path to freedom.

In Conversation with Dianne Tidball

An author and pastor, Dianne Tidball is currently the regional minister of the East Midland Baptist Association in England.

What most encourages you in your work with pastors and churches?

There are toxic situations in church life and these can overwhelm us, so we do need to be reminded of the good things that are going on. The encouragements include communities small and large who understand that the Bible is the truth of God, and when they live it out see God working by his Spirit. Leading on from this, I am encouraged by pastors who have the simple yet profound priority of teaching and applying the Bible and from this see changed lives, transformed communities and spiritual and numerical growth. I am also encouraged by leaders who intentionally preach and teach biblical truth and then live that teaching out in their leadership, reflecting God's kingdom values of grace, generosity, servanthood and hope.

I am encouraged by God's people living out God's love in the community in which God has placed them. Every church group is made up of people who have insecurities, differences of opinion and burdens they carry. When those flawed people learn to live in forgiveness, love and kindness as they worship God and witness to God's salvation in Christ, that is more than encouraging: it is inspirational. The most powerful tool for mission we have today is communities living out the values of the kingdom of God.

In working with pastors my particular encouragement is seeing gifted men and women seeking to be Christ-centred. There are so many pressures to be successful, to be self-seeking and self-preserving that when those who lead do so in humility and trust in God, seeking God's best when that is costly to themselves, it is greatly heartening.

What warning signs cause you to become concerned about someone's leadership?

A lack of love for the people they lead is a worrying sign in a Christian leader. It is fundamental that we want God's best for people because we love them and care for them. People will very quickly sense if a pastor is using them to build up his or her reputation and image rather than having a genuine love for the people God has called them to shepherd.

Continuing ministerial development is a prerequisite to being energized and effective in ministry. However, there are those who go to far too many conferences and are always reading books and having the latest ideas, but never actually get on with doing the leading and engaging with people. Also worrying are those who are isolationist and who don't gather with other ministers and share burdens and challenges; who don't keep their spiritual energy through receiving the ministry of others and being renewed.

Perhaps the most worrying sign of toxic flaws in leadership is lack of character and insecurity. Shallow character leads to self-protection, arrogance and self-preservation, which are a disaster in leadership meetings and church meetings, and in the daily support and encouragement of others. Those who constantly need affirmation, status and power to make up for their deep flaws can survive in the short term on personality and gifting, but in the long term such issues can be corrosive for a church community.

Any ideas on how change can be best managed in churches?

This is the big issue for churches in the UK today. Change can be managed effectively when people feel secure in God and his greatness, and in the leadership of the church. Keeping people conscious of God's love, grace and power is essential alongside respect for people's anxieties, history and uncertainties as we introduce change. Good leadership will introduce change carefully, thoughtfully and prayerfully with love for the people, taking time to inform and maintaining communication of the vision of where the changes will lead. Any change can lead to negative comments and misunderstandings; the ability to receive these without being defensive, to respond thoughtfully and not to give more credence to such things than is helpful, is an aspect of effective change management.

Managing change takes risk, courage and clarity. There is the risk that if the congregation does not follow, the leader's reputation may be undermined. Courage is needed to gently challenge power bases within congregations. Clarity is needed to keep the focus of the change at the centre of planning and thinking. Much change is complex; it is about changing a culture and giving value to the past while moving forward.

How do you decide if a call to sacrifice is appropriate or exploitative?

As you suggest in the question, sacrifice is crucial in discipleship and Christian leadership, but there are times when that willingness to lay down our lives for the sake of the gospel is exploited for the sake of an organization or human institution. A call to sacrifice is potentially appropriate when a community, together, forfeit money or security for the sake of a vision to fulfil God's calling. If only one person is expected to make the major part of the sacrifice while others don't, that would be exploitative. The language used in seeking sacrifice can be indicative of whether the sacrifice is appropriate – those who keep suggesting 'God will provide' with no indication of how are in denial of responsibilities and fellowship. I would encourage anyone entering into an arrangement of serving a church and expecting even modest remuneration to have the expectations clearly stated in writing; it will save a lot of pain later.

An exploitative call to sacrifice will have an element of misleading people who were encouraged to think one thing when the reality was something else; or they would feel manipulated or pressurized into being sacrificial. In some churches, emotional blackmail is prevalent. On the other hand, sacrifice for the sake of the kingdom of God is essential to our discipleship, and in our consumer culture we have to resist all temptations to avoid sacrifice and to be self-serving.

To Ponder and Discuss

1. Have you benefited from the leadership of a pastor who was a servant, shepherd and steward? What did you find most helpful about their leadership? Have you thanked them for it?
2. Reread the list of ten signs that leadership is at risk of going astray. Are any of these dangers present in your own setting? If so, can you do anything about it? Would you add any signs to this list? If so, what are they?
3. Reflect on the potential tension between the best interests of the group and the interests of the individual. Can you think of a time when you faced this dilemma? How was it resolved? Are there lessons to be learnt and things you would do again; or alternatively, things you would not repeat?
4. Look again at Nieuwhof's list of nine signs that indicate a risk of burnout. Do any apply to you or to someone you know? If so, what steps can be taken to help?

7

Contours for a Transforming Christian World View

The Link between Belief and Lifestyle

It's the chicken or egg question. Does what we believe impact the way we live, or is it that the way we live shapes what we are willing to believe? In all likelihood, it is a bit of both.

I still remember the preacher's startling claim. He had been browsing through *Playboy* magazine (that certainly grabbed my attention) and had been surprised to discover an article entitled 'God Is Dead'. While he didn't agree with the author's conclusion, he had to concede that the article was well written and carefully thought through. As he said, 'Not the sort of article you expect to find in *Playboy* magazine.' He then followed it through with a statement that has remained with me: 'But then, if you adopt a *Playboy* lifestyle, you need to believe that God is dead.' He then suggested that this is the thesis of Psalm 14:1, where the psalmist writes, 'The fool says in his heart, "There is no God." They are corrupt, their deeds are vile; there is no one who does good.' This is a description of functional atheism, rather than its ideological or academic version. The psalmist's argument is that because a certain lifestyle has been adopted, people choose to live as though there is no God to give account to, which is indeed foolish.

It works the other way around as well. If we do believe in God's existence, and also believe that we will give an account for our lives, we will watch our lifestyle and behaviour more carefully.

While this much is not controversial, what happens when what we believe is faulty? Does flawed belief lead to a damaged lifestyle? And is the reverse also true: that a damaged lifestyle will lead to flawed belief? If there is a relationship between the two (and it seems likely that there is), it is possible that one cause of toxic faith is a defective grasp of the faith.

In this chapter I will try to outline some of the common unhelpful traps into which people often fall when they think of the Christian faith. Implicit in the critique is what I consider to be a wholesome and winsome understanding of the Christian faith – a portrayal that is both orthodox and biblical.

Most train stations have a sign urging patrons to 'mind the gap'. It is just a little step from the platform onto the train, but if it is mismanaged the consequences are serious. In a similar manner we might almost get the point of many of the main doctrines of the Christian faith; the problem is caused by the gap.[1]

Let me be clear: while it is untrue to suggest that only those who obtain high distinctions in theology are adequately equipped to follow Jesus, sometimes the gap in our understanding produces unintended but negative consequences. Take the difference between law and grace. Viewing Christ-following as an ethical mandate consisting of a lengthy list of 'do this' and 'don't do that' statements might give the impression that we hold the moral high ground and can claim to be virtuous. The downside is that it leaves us in a similar position to the Pharisees of old – and Jesus didn't seem to be especially fond of them.

When does the gap between a biblical world view and our own become a serious problem? Think of the consequences when we strike the wrong note with any of the following . . .

Six Common Problem Areas

1. When we sweat the 'how' of creation instead of the 'why'

Steeped as we are in the scientific method of the last few centuries, our instinct on reading the opening chapters of Genesis is often to mutter a 'hardly likely' to its claim of a six-day creation. While we would acknowledge that the detail provided is scant, we are unlikely to instinctively assume that every detail must be literally embraced.

For some this becomes deeply problematic, and they either reject the Christian faith as a result, or they go to extraordinary lengths to try to establish that the Genesis creation account is in fact compatible with the discoveries of modern science. While they sometimes succeed in convincing themselves, that conviction rarely extends to those they attempt to persuade. An unfortunate impasse results. On the one side is a small group of devotees who believe that they have reconciled science and the Bible; on the other are a group who smugly chortle at what they consider to be an example of intellectual and scientific suicide. The latter quickly relegate the Genesis account to a waste basket of quaint but irrelevant myths from antiquity.

I would like to suggest that this is an exceptionally unfruitful approach and does a disservice to the biblical text, largely because it arbitrarily tries to force the Bible to answer questions of recent interest rather than the truly significant questions the original authors set out to answer.

So what questions does Genesis answer? Here are a few – and don't miss how profound each is.

- Is there a God?
- Is this an accidental or intentional universe?
- What is God's relationship to the creation?
- Why is the world simultaneously wonderful and dreadful?
- What is the purpose of life?
- What responsibilities do humans have in the stewardship of this planet?
- What does it mean to be human?

To avoid creating a false antithesis between science and the Bible, it helps to acknowledge that the Bible does not answer the question 'How was the world made?' in such a way as to render a scientific investigation of the question redundant.

Although the Bible does not focus on 'how' the world was made, it does answer a question most find more compelling – 'why' the world was made. When we focus on the question 'how', we usually land up in silliness, attempting to appear knowledgeable in areas where we have little expertise. By contrast, when we focus on the 'why' question we articulate answers of profound depth. They literally transform the way in which we see and understand the world. The answers we offer to the 'why' question are filled with hope and meaning. If accepted, they change the world for the good.

2. When we idealize or vilify humanity

Colliding truths are usually both true, even if unpacking is required. Take these two. People are essentially noble and good. They can be trusted – indeed, they are just 'a little lower than the angels', to quote the psalmist (Ps. 8:5). People are also villainous, cruel and depraved. If you ask 'Can both of these contradictory descriptions be true?' the answer is 'yes'. Genesis explains how.

On the one hand, the Bible affirms that people are made in the image of God. This staggering truth is hard to take in. Theologians debate at length what is meant by the claim. The intention to create humanity in God's image is proclaimed in Genesis 1:26, with verse 27 signing off on the success of the project. As both men and women are made in the image of God, it is clear that the image has nothing to do with gender – a rather radical insight for a text written in a world where patriarchy dominated.

It is hard to overestimate the loftiness of the claim that humans are made in God's image. Implications that arise from it flow thick and fast. Although much of human history has been a reflection of our inability to live up to the creation mandate, the responsibility and privilege of being an image bearer remain.

Being made in God's image is a statement about our identity – and the identity of every other human being. It affirms that we belong to God. The theologian Helmut Thielicke expands on what Luther called the *dignitas aliena* (alien dignity) when he writes:

> The only question is whether I can see the whole person if I do not see him in his relationship to God and therefore as the bearer of an 'alien dignity'. If I am blind to this dimension, then I can only give the other person a partial dignity insofar as I estimate his importance 'for me' – even if this includes far more than his mere *functional* importance for me! – but not insofar as I see his importance 'for God'.[2]

We only fully confer the worth each person deserves when we remember that all people are made in the image of God and therefore have inestimable value. Sadly, this truth has been one that we have sometimes forgotten. When we fail to stand up for the rights of the marginalized and oppressed we imply that they are lesser humans. We close our eyes to their status as image bearers, and in doing so embrace a version of faith that is sub-Christian.

It is true to say that humans are made in the image of God. It is, however, an incomplete truth. When a partial truth masquerades as a complete truth it is in danger of becoming an untruth. A fuller account has to delve deeper into the creation story, and discovers in that narrative the explanation for the otherwise inexplicable cruelty and savagery shown by the human race. While humanity initially flourished in the garden of Eden, the day came when they disobeyed the instruction to refrain from eating from the fruit of the tree of the knowledge of good and evil. While we could debate the deeper significance of that act, perhaps we can simplify many arguments by noting that in their quest to differentiate between good and evil, they staked their autonomy from God. After eating from that tree they hoped to decide what was good and what was not without any reference to God. This is the heart of human sin – the pull away from God, the desire for self-sufficiency, to know right and wrong without any need to refer back to God.[3]

Similarly, humanity is condemned for its attempt to build the tower of Babel – the account is found in Genesis 11. A superficial

   When Faith Turns Ugly

reading of the passage leaves most confused. Why is God so annoyed by this attempt to build a tower to reach heaven? Granted, it was a misguided quest. After all, this was the ancient world, and any tower was unlikely to be more than a few storeys high – no doubt impressive to our ancestors, but paltry in comparison with the skyscrapers of today. The problem with the tower had nothing to do with its height or its mistaken notion that heaven is up in the sky. The issue was the underlying attitude behind the project. At heart, the tower of Babel was an attempt to reach heaven unaided, and thus to render God obsolete.

The attempt to stake autonomy from God is the essence of the fall of humanity. We are made in God's image. When we try to dispense with the need for God, we sever ourselves from the one in whose image we are made. This is to shake our fist at God and to say that we no longer wish to be who we are – creatures made in God's image. It is the reason for the pervasive sadness that is never far from the surface of life. Something has gone awry. We no longer reflect the image of the God who made us. We have embarked on a misguided journey to create an alternative identity for ourselves. We are trying to become who we are not.

3. When grace is trivialized to legalism

In the light of humanity's decision to stake its autonomy from God, God could have accepted the insult and decided to have nothing more to do with our rebellious ancestors. Instead, God continues to strive with the human race, demonstrating a willingness to do whatever it takes to ensure that people come to their senses and reclaim their status as those who bear the image of the God who made them. The 'whatever it takes' turned out to be extremely costly. It took the form of the cross at Calvary.

Why did God do this? We should not answer too quickly, lest it imply that what God did was totally understandable and predictable. Actually, it was anything but. In trying to find an adequate word to describe it, theologians have settled upon a little word with an astonishing depth of meaning: grace.

Ever since humanity deliberately defied God and severed the close relational tie they had previously enjoyed with their Creator, the universe has limped along awkwardly. To be sure, there have been moments of brilliance. As humans we should not think too highly of ourselves. Even our incomprehensible disobedience was not enough to totally ruin the good world that God made. The fingerprints of the goodness of God remain everywhere. But our rebellion has left deep scars. Things go wrong – sometimes devastatingly wrong.

When things go wrong and someone is clearly to blame, a common response is to ask what should happen to the person at fault. The Bible explores a few options.

Option one is the instinctive one. If someone does something wrong, punish them so severely that anyone tempted to follow their example will immediately eliminate the possibility from their mind. There is a troubling account found in Genesis 4:23–4. A man by the name of Lamech is injured by a younger man. While the detail provided is scant, we are told that in retaliation for this injury Lamech kills the younger man, thereafter boasting to his two wives, Adah and Zillah, of his feat. The implication of his victory song is clear. Do the slightest thing against me and I will obliterate you. It is a sure way to escalate conflict and to guarantee that any relational breakdown remains irreparable. With this model, the enemy remains enemy for ever.

To soften this instinctive response, when the law was given to Moses, a system was put in place to limit retaliation to the extent of the offence. Put simply, the eye for eye (or tooth for tooth) principle was championed. Among other places it can be found in Exodus 21:23–25. It was a helpful advance. Rather than escalate violence, the eye for eye principle restricted it. It was a neat and tidy system. If someone broke your arm, you could break theirs. You could not, however, break their neck. That would be far more serious than the offence they had committed against you and would violate this tit for tat system.

While 'eye for eye' was better than Lamech's endless revenge, it had its limitations. Most notable was that it was powerless to reconcile warring parties. If someone broke your toe, and you carefully retaliated by breaking theirs, you might feel avenged for the wrong done against you, but it was unlikely that afterwards you would hug and suggest drinks at the local pub! More likely you would continue to glare at the offender and growl, 'So don't ever do that again!' before you both hobbled off, trying to mask the pain from your broken bones.

It took the brilliance of Jesus to suggest an alternative model. Now, there is no doubting that in some ways Jesus' instruction sounds remarkably naive. Perhaps you remember the drift of the argument in the Sermon on the Mount (Matt. 5:43–8). Rather than retaliating, Jesus suggests that we don't attempt to resist those who do evil against us. Jesus earths his teaching with a challenging example. If someone has just struck us on the right cheek, we should turn the left cheek to them. He goes on to inform us that, instead of limiting love to our neighbour, we should extend it to our enemy as well.

At a certain level this sounds like madness. You can imagine what Lamech's response would have been – 'Never in a thousand years!' is the mild version! Yet two thousand years before Ghandi, Jesus recognized the power of non-retaliation. More than that, he recognized the transforming power of forgiveness. If we refuse to hold something against another, especially if we are perfectly entitled to be offended, we open the door through which the enemy can walk and become a friend. They do not have to fight the layers of our angry resentment before they can reach us. We are open to friendship with them, even while they are raging against us.

Why would we do this? The little word 'grace' springs to mind. As people who bear the image of the God who made us, we know that we are made for relationship with one another. If we close our heart to another, even if they have wronged us, we fall short of who we are made to be.

Opening our heart to those who reject us is a high-risk strategy. The cross of Calvary underlines this truth emphatically. Paradoxically it is the very 'failure' of the approach that is its success. The mystery of the Christian faith is this: when we most reject the God who made us (and it is hard to imagine a greater 'we don't want you' than a crucifixion), we are the closest to re-entering into relationship with our Maker. Jesus' attitude and actions on the cross were so unexpected that the Roman centurion who had overseen his crucifixion was overwhelmed to the point that he was heard to exclaim, 'Surely this man was the Son of God' (Mark 15:39). What caused the change? We can't know for sure. Perhaps it was Jesus' plea, 'Father, forgive them, for they do not know what they are doing' (Luke 23:34). Perhaps it was simply Jesus' trust and courage in the midst of extreme suffering. While our rebellion against God has marred the image we were created in, it is not so damaged as to be incapable of recognizing that through the cross, God invites us to find forgiveness and a restored relationship with our Creator. Why does God go to such extraordinary lengths to be in relationship with us? It is inexplicable, but that little word 'grace' is a start.

While this thumbnail sketch of grace is far from complete, I want simply to underline how sad it is when we allow this astonishing grace to morph into legalism. Too often, we try to replace grace by a trite set of rules and regulations that suggest that being in relationship with God is about ticking whatever seem to be the really important moral boxes of our time. Depending on our context, that could mean anything from dressing in a certain way (usually making a virtue of the dreary), refraining from dancing, being shocked at the sexual struggles of others, having really boring Sundays or opposing anything new. None of these has anything to do with grace, but they do leave us in charge of writing our own rules and appearing to win the right to a permanent audience with God as a result of our moral rectitude.

4. When the Trinity is about maths instead of community

Say the word 'Trinity' to the average Christian and their eyes glaze over as they prepare for a confusing explanation of how it is that God can appear to be three (Father, Son and Spirit) while actually being only one God. Most draw on imperfect analogies – it is like H_2O which is always H_2O but can be a solid (ice), liquid (water) or gas (steam). Others suggest it is like an egg which is made up of a shell, yolk and the albumen. And then there is Augustine's grammatical argument. God is the highest love, but in order to have love, there must be a lover, a loved, and the action of love. In order to be love, God must at the same time be the object, the subject and the verb, and thus have three parts. Yup – it's not too hard to understand why those eyes glaze over. It is inevitable when we treat the Trinity as a mathematical improbability which we have to justify and explain.

So how should we think of the Trinity – and does it matter?

The revealed God is triune. The mathematical complexity of demonstrating that one plus one plus one equals one has proved a theological red herring. The only God we can know is the God who is revealed and we can safely assume that God is as God is revealed – one essence in three persons. So we must work with what we know. The revealed God is never an isolated, lonely God, but comes to us in the rich relational life of Father, Son and Spirit. We are told that humans are made in the image of God, and we can argue that our life calling is to live up to the image in which we have been made. To image such a God would therefore presumably require a comparable rich communal life in the entity that we call church. At the very least, the triune God is a rebuke to excessive individualism, especially if it comes at the expense of the life of the community. That a strong stress on the individual, often at the expense of the communal, has been a characteristic of many churches should be of concern to us.[4]

It starts with an emphasis on individual salvation which is pivotal to the evangelical movement.[5] It continues in the music of the movement. 'My Jesus, I love you, I know Thou art mine' is not really in accord with the prayer Jesus taught his followers, which begins not with the 'my' word but with the 'our' word – 'Our Father in heaven' (Matt. 6:9). Now, a warm intimate relationship with our Father is entirely appropriate, but when it is emphasized at the expense of our communal life, something is amiss.

In Ephesians 3 Paul reminds us of two conditions that help the church to partially comprehend the width, length, height and depth of Christ's love for us. The first is that 'Christ may dwell in your hearts through faith' so that we would be 'rooted and established in love'; which naturally leads to the second, which is of us being 'together with all the Lord's holy people' in the communal quest to discover the love that 'surpasses knowledge'. All this is a world away from the drift towards what Alan Jamieson calls 'churchless faith'.[6] The problem with churchless faith is that 'together with all the Lord's holy people' simply disappears. The lonely self embarked on the 'me, myself and I' quest to discover God is quickly pulled up when the realization dawns that this God is triune. The self cannot enter into a one-on-one relationship with God, for the one it attempts to relate to is three. The self is immediately thrust into community.

This is not to suggest that the self disappears in community. Again, the triune nature of God helps us avoid this potential trap. The Father is not the Son, the Son is not the Spirit, the Spirit is not the Father. Rather than the disappearance of the self, the self is most truly self in relationship, in community. Outside of community, the self cannot image the God whose likeness it is invited to reflect.

Life-serving faith grasps that relationship with the triune God thrusts us into transforming community life. There are no solitary Christians. We belong to God and so we belong to each other.

5. When stewardship means exploitation and the status quo is sanctified

The opening chapters of the Bible paint an exciting picture of the task facing the human race. Having been made in the image of their Creator, they are to be stewards of God's creation, ensuring that they build a world where every plant and creature can be fruitful and multiply. One of the stunning portraits in Genesis 2 is found in verses 19–20. God invites Adam to name the birds and animals. The scene captures the imagination. God actively brings each bird and animal to Adam to see what he will name them. The Creator of all does not interfere in this process, for we are told that whatever name Adam selected, that was its name.

Think of the importance of names. A poorly chosen name can prove a heavy burden. Some nicknames are specifically chosen for their cruelty – Fatty, Dumbo . . . the list could go on. We often become what we are named. I was born a few weeks early, a significantly underweight and vulnerable infant. But my parents named me Brian, which means 'strong'. I like to think that they were right and that, in spite of initial appearances, this was my invitation to be who I could be – someone with some resilient strength. Names in the Bible are often changed, Abram, Sarai, Jacob and Simon being some examples of those whose original names were considered by God to not adequately reflect the call and potential of their lives.

If names are so significant, the responsibility of naming creation should not be underestimated. Surely this was a task that could only be performed by one who was an image bearer of the Creator – for great creativity is required to name appropriately. God's was the first creation, but in delegating the task of naming to image bearers, God assigned humanity the task of building a world with a suitable name – one that reflects all the potential inherent in the original creation. The concept gives me goose bumps. Such an incredible and exciting responsibility! Imagine being caught up in a story where the main theme line is 'building a world with a better name'.

Building a world with a better name – such a lofty mandate; but in our current world our experienced reality is that names are allowed to divide (name any ethnic group, and the name causes angst or ridicule in another), and some names have been allowed to disappear, some species now extinct because of our neglect of the creation mandate. Sadly the church, out of a misguided attempt to safeguard the status quo, has sometimes been complicit in this, with conservative agendas being allowed to trump most calls for innovation. Many recent calls for change have been motivated by a desire to build a world with a better name, but have often been hushed into silence by people of faith who have failed to grasp the dynamic implications of their original directive.

Life-serving faith requires Christ-followers to ponder and then act upon their delegated responsibility to find new and better names for a world where so many names jar and bring out the worst in us.

6. *When eschatology becomes escapism instead of enticing invitation*

In Chapter 3 I wrote of the risk of trivializing eschatology so that thoughts of the future take on apocalyptic dimensions that enthral and fascinate us rather than challenging us to lead lives in the present moment which are worthy of and consistent with the future to which we are called. We do indeed wait for a new earth, but the fact that it is an earth renewed rather than obliterated is a perpetual reminder of the validity of the first creation. God's intention with the first creation will not be abandoned. To the contrary, it will be fulfilled. Paul informs us in Colossians 1:17 that 'in him [Jesus] all things hold together'. Ultimately, all things will find their resolution and be reconciled in Jesus. All our actions in the present should be shaped by and be consistent with this hope.

This willingness to allow our future reality to shape present reality should see Christ-followers marching to a tune that is markedly different from those around them. It requires great courage to do this. We need to ask if each project we embark upon has been birthed from faith, hope and love – for 1 Corinthians 13:13 assures us that these are the qualities that will remain for ever. A world where we embrace that which flows from faith, hope and love prepares us well for a new heaven and a new earth. It is eschatology at its best, and has nothing to do with speculation about time lines or the sequence of the rapture.

Piecing This Together

At its best, theology leads to doxology – the praise and worship of God. Too often, we allow theological reflection to degenerate into a game of 'caught you', where we delightedly quibble about the misrepresentation of some theological position. While such debates might keep us mentally alert, they rarely feed the soul. A holistic Christian world view unites three 'ortho's together – orthodoxy, orthopraxy and orthopathy – as we will see in the next chapter. Right thinking about God is only credible when it is backed by right practice and right feeling. When these three come together, the doxology can truly be sung, for the God who transforms our thinking, acting and feeling is the God of the Bible, and is the God who commands our love, worship and adoration.

The way to avoid toxic faith is to embrace life-serving faith. Life-serving faith is close at hand when we dive into the why of creation, the depth of grace, the mystery of being an image bearer, the glory of being able to relate to the triune God and the challenge of building a world with a better name, and when we live in the light of the hope that this world will be made new. Never settle for lesser versions of faith.

In Conversation with Stephen O'Doherty

Stephen O'Doherty is a former shadow minister in the New South Wales Parliament and is currently the CEO of Christian Schools Australia, a peak educational body representing over 150 Australian schools.

Stephen, you gave up a promising career in politics to further the cause of Christian schooling. In what way do Christian schools build a world with a better name?

It is easy for people to be cynical about politics, but as one long-standing MP once told me, 'The trouble with politicians is that they will keep on acting as human beings.'

I was acutely aware of two things. Despite many heroic and noble efforts, humanity so often fails to consistently be the best that it can be. Yet we yearn to live up to that standard! To use your wonderful phrase, we instinctively know the name of the world we aspire to build. At the same moment, we realize our own inadequacy to build it.

In Australia we are fortunate indeed to live under the rule of law in a Westminster-style democracy. Yet every time I stood to debate some piece of legislation or another, or discuss a shift in government policy, I realized that even with the immense power to make the laws that govern society, the most we could do as a parliament was to attempt to regulate behaviour. We could not legislate to change the human heart. Law alone is insufficient to make the world a better place.

The power to regulate and govern is not insignificant. It must be used wisely and only for the benefit of others. But the real power to build a better name for our society lies with those doing the building and naming. A better world only comes when individuals are formed, or transformed, to live a life that makes a difference, following the example of Jesus, and fulfilling our original mandate to be men and women after God's own heart (because we are made in his image). And we need to know the name we are aspiring to.

As a policy maker I could see very clearly the crucial role played by formal (compulsory school) education in the spiritual and moral formation of individuals and hence society. As a Christian I understood that this role is mandated to the institutions of family and church. Yet, with these institutions under great pressure, we have both an opportunity and an obligation to work through Christian schooling in order to see young people educated and formed with a clear understanding that their life's purpose is best found by following Christ's teachings and example, and to work in his name as radical transformers of society: active participants in their democracy, understanding that they are saved by grace, finding joy and fulfilment in service, and energetically working in the world for godly outcomes; with standards of behaviour that honour the dignity with which we are all created, justice for the oppressed and marginalized, and a radical care for the world and others that places individual greed in last place.

In short, while it was a big (and slightly unpopular) decision to resign my seat in parliament, my hope was that by working to strengthen, grow and support Christian education, I would in some way contribute to others taking their place not just in parliaments, but in leadership positions throughout the community, to follow Christ and transform our society.

Some might say that Christian schools represent an escape from the world and inoculate their students from facing the harder issues of life. Do you think that is true?

Most parents want to protect their children from harm. If they are not thinking carefully about the moral, intellectual, spiritual and cultural influences on their growing children, they should be! These things should not be left to chance. Christian or not, parents make deliberate choices about the level of engagement with the broader culture they allow their children. As those children grow to maturity, we naturally expand their cultural engagement. Governments recognize this principle through age-based content-rating systems for movies and TV. Even Facebook has an age minimum.

Paul rather aptly describes the Christian life as a journey to maturity, personally and corporately (1 Cor. 13:11; Eph. 4:13).

The role of the Christian school is, with parents and the church, to help students on their journey to spiritual maturity, while developing their intellectual, physical, social and emotional growth. Such growth is a natural part of the community life of Christ-followers. According to Ephesians 4 (incidentally, the passage most responsible for me entering public life as a parliamentarian), to become more like Christ is to mature. In the process Christ's church is built, as each person uses their gifts in mutual service, and the end result is that the Christian community stands out – it is substantially different from the culture around it. I see this as the call on every believer, and on the community of believers, to show leadership to a world that is very much in need of hearing and seeing the truth in love and in action.

We are to live in light of the future, of which we have an assurance. Or as it has been put so well in the preceding pages: our present actions are to be shaped by our eschatology, consistent with the hope that we profess.

I hope it is clear – at least, it is clear to me – that what follows from this is an obligation and biblical responsibility to equip young people with the discernment and spiritual maturity to be culture-shapers, to engage in the work of transformation that has been entrusted to us; to help them to have a crystal-clear world view, an understanding of what they believe and why, and a passion for making changes consistent with their faith in Christ. This is quantifiable and different from a more monastic approach of cultural inoculation.

What were some of the special challenges you faced as a Christian politician trying to represent Christ in a fairly brutal environment?

The NSW Parliament is known as 'the Bear Pit', and not without good reason. Democracy there is often played out through blistering debates and 'winner takes all' tribalism.

You will not be surprised to learn that one of the biggest challenges was to maintain relationships despite political differences (on both sides of the Chamber!). Less obvious, perhaps, was the challenge of what I might call 'finding your true voice' in an environment where so many people want you to fulfil their expectations.

As a Christian, the danger is to let cultural norms become a proxy for clear Christian thinking. This is the danger that is highlighted in this chapter on the 'contours' of a life lived in faith. Think for a moment about an issue as complex as drug-law reform. Which policy response is most Christlike – harm minimization or a hardline 'war on drugs' approach? This can be argued both ways, even by Christian believers of good standing with an identical theology regarding the sanctity of every human life.

Finding a policy ethic that explicates Christian principles and turns them into good public policy for a broken world: that is the problem at hand; and doing so with integrity in a way that is not captive to this or that pressure group or sectional interest is the challenge.

You've always had a special concern for people with disabilities. Why is that, and why do you think their cause should be championed?

One of the greatest joys of being a local member was to experience a *bigger* side to community life than most people get to experience. I became particularly close, and still am, to a disability service in my electorate, Studio ARTES (I remain their patron). One of the many great things about Studio ARTES is that it creates ways for people with a disability to rightfully make their contribution to enrich the community.

As a Christian I see it like this: my world is not complete unless people with a disability, made in the image of God, are fully part of it. The Christian faith makes some very significant claims on me at this point. First, my brother or sister with a disability is to be understood, loved and cherished *as they are*. They are made in the image of God, and derive their dignity from his love for them. A friend with cerebral palsy despairs that almost every time she goes to a new church, well-meaning but very unhelpful people come up and want to pray for her healing. She will be healed – in heaven. We *all* will be made new. For now, she wants to be seen for what she is and known for the contribution only she can make.

Second, people with a disability deserve nothing less than to be fully included in our community life, including in the life of the church. If we don't know how to do that, we must learn.

Third, if there are barriers and injustices that stand in the way to a more inclusive community, we are obliged to work to eliminate them. This will include active advocacy, and may include personal involvement in the political process! Many Christian schools are shining examples of inclusion, despite a funding shortfall that directly works against full choice of school for students with a disability. This is currently a top policy priority of our movement.

To Ponder and Discuss

1. Do you agree that what we believe impacts how we live? If so, identify the way in which some of your core beliefs impact your behaviour.
2. What do you think are the dangers of thinking either too highly of humanity or of underestimating our worth?
3. Does grace mean that anything goes? When does costly grace become cheap grace?
4. In your sphere of influence, what might it mean to build a world with a better name?
5. Theology leads to doxology. Spend some time thanking God for life-serving faith.

8

Life-Serving Faith: Transformed Individuals

The Big Picture

Up until now, much of this book has focused on why faith sometimes turns ugly. We have looked at destructive versions of faith and have issued the appropriate warnings. However, knowing what to avoid is never enough. We also need a clear sense of what it is that we are called to embrace. This chapter therefore starts with the big picture that undergirds the Christian faith – the overarching narrative that guides and directs us. Once we deeply grasp this story, we are in a position to explore its potential to change individuals for good (which is the focus of this chapter) and then how it transforms communities (the focus of Chapter 9).

The opening portrait in the biblical account of creation is one where a creative God decides to bring about something that did not previously exist, and in doing so builds something to which he can ascribe a satisfied 'and it was good' evaluation.[1] This reaches a new height after the creation of Adam and Eve. After this creation the author of Genesis informs us that 'God saw all that he had made, and it was very good' (Gen. 1:31). We are therefore not simply looking at a good creation, but one which is *very* good. Is such an enthusiastic assessment justified?

In considering your answer, think of the portrait of the world painted in the opening chapters of Genesis. It is a deeply relational world. The setting is an idyllic garden filled with fruit-bearing trees, each well watered by the river that runs through it.

This garden was visited regularly by the God who made it and who communicated with the original couple as they went about their task of representing God (or being the image or icon of God) to the rest of the created order. Animals and birds were not anonymous objects in this garden, for each had been named by the first human created. The diet appears to have been vegetarian, meaning that no living creature had to fear being eaten by another. Indeed, it seems that death had no part in the original scheme of things. Work was, however, necessary – but this was not the work of a later post-fall era, for at this stage labour represented creative tending of the good world that God had made. It was pleasurable.

Clothing was unnecessary, and Adam and Eve formed and occupied the first nudist colony, being completely at ease with the bodies God had given them. We are not told whether these bodies were short or tall, fat or thin, hairy or bald, clear-skinned or spotted; and the absence of this information perhaps indicates its irrelevance in a world where shame caused by unfavourable comparison was not a feature.

The first human was made from the dust of the earth and the breath of God. There is something deeply poetic about this. Frailty and majestic otherness reside together in Adam. He is indeed the dust of the earth, but he is also made from the breath of God. As if to emphasize this, a tree, placed in the very centre of the garden, bears fruit which the original couple are forbidden to eat. Perhaps if the tree had been located at the outskirts of the garden it could have been overlooked. Many don't wander to the very borders of their property; but how can you ignore something at the very centre? Its message was clear. As image bearers, obedience to the God who made them was not compelled, but invited. They were always free to choose the other, for how could they be like God if they had no capacity for independent action? The choice to obey was always theirs, and the centrally located tree was a constant reminder that another option was within their grasp.

Not that the temptation to disobey was strong. The picture painted in Genesis 1 and 2 is of death-defying, vegetarian nudists – a delightful community where all are known, named and comfortable with their existence. Innocence dominates, and there are no sour experiences to cause any troubled dreams. No doubt each night's sleep was simply a pleasant interlude before the start of another day in paradise.

Those familiar with narrative theory will recognize the classic plot-like structure. We begin with the ideal, but a threat is never far from the surface. In Genesis chapter 3, this emerges with force. The simple existence of the tree of the knowledge of good and evil had not launched Adam and Eve into rebellion, but this changes when a crafty serpent suggests that a desire to restrict, rather than kindliness, lies behind God's instruction that they leave this fruit untasted. The temptation is succumbed to, and the narrative theme shifts from paradise to paradise lost.

And what losses they are. On eating the fruit, the eyes of Adam and Eve are opened in such a way that what they see no longer delights, but brings a sense of shame – a realization of nakedness. For the first time, the body is viewed negatively. Not only do they feel a need to hide their bodies behind clothes made from fig leaves, they now wish to hide their very selves from the God who had made them. As God walks through the garden searching for them, a question is needed: 'Where are you?' The portrait is poignant. Adam and Eve are no longer innocents rushing to a caring parent, but guilty rebels, aware they have done something of magnitude. The instinct to embrace has been replaced by a gulf of alienation.

The severed human–divine relationship is quickly replicated in a strained husband–wife relationship. When asked if their clothing and hiding indicates that they have eaten from the forbidden fruit, Adam decides that attack is the best form of defence. Genesis 3:12 records his reply: 'The woman you put here with me – she gave me some fruit from the tree, and I ate it.' In other words, 'God, this is your fault. You made the woman (did I ask you for her?), and now she has led me astray. Clearly the two of you are to blame . . .'

Eve adopts a similar strategy, though she suggests that the fault should be placed at the serpent's door.

Would the outcome have been different if the instinct of our ancestors had been to cry out, 'I and I only am to blame. Lord, have mercy'? We cannot know, for clearly this was not their response.

A different order dawns. The door of paradise is closed, work becomes difficult and joyless, childbirth is painful and dangerous, and male–female relationships change and become about desire and dominance.

Not that grace is absent even from this first portrait of disobedience. Aware that Adam and Eve are about to enter a hostile new order, God clothes them in something more substantial than fig leaves. They exit the garden clothed in the skins of animals. Though punishing them for their rebellion, God is committed to their survival. The cost is great. Death has entered the world, and Adam and Eve are protected from the elements by the animals that have died on their behalf. A theme of substitution is introduced. The animals they named are now victims of our ancestors' disobedience.

If the Bible is a story with plot and purpose, it passes through the usual three stages that undergird most narratives. After the opening stage where the scene is set and life is portrayed in its ideal form, we move rapidly into stage two, which in most narratives is where a problem is introduced and developed. Hopes of easy resolution are explored but invariably turn out to be ineffective, and the complexity of the problem grows with each aborted attempt at a solution.

The Bible is no exception to this classic structure, and the lengthy second stage explores the impact of human sin, and attempts to resolve it. One crisis follows another. God chooses a nation and gives it laws to abide by. This nation is to be a light to all others, and to point them to the path that leads to peace with God, the neighbour and creation. However, the chosen nation, Israel, rather than adhere to the law they have been given, routinely abandon it. Punishment follows to varying degrees, and often leads to a temporary repentance and a fresh compliance, but the change is never long-lived. The drama grows until God sends his own Son to point people back to a path of obedience and relationship with him. Rather than changing everything, it leads to a yet greater act of rebellion against God. The human race crucifies God's Son, Jesus. At this stage it seems as though this narrative is a tragedy. Rather than the problem being resolved, it has escalated dramatically, with the human race adding to its shortfall the execution of the son of their Creator.

This, then, is a narrative without the usual third stage, that of resolution. Except . . . except that, as in the greatest narratives, when we have given up in despair, the impossible suddenly becomes possible. The crucified Jesus conquers death (the terrible consequence of the first rebellion) and returns to commission his followers to continue his mission in the world. This will not be an unaccompanied journey, for although Jesus will return to his Father, he will ensure that his followers are empowered by the Holy Spirit to do what would otherwise prove impossible. Great adventures lie ahead, and to date, two thousand years of church history have unfolded. While responding to the Spirit's leading in the mission of transforming the world, Christ-followers engage in tasks that need to be done, but also face an inner journey. As offspring of the first Adam, they discover within their own being a similar bent towards rebellion and evil. While the consequences of this bent were removed through the crucifixion and resurrection of Jesus, the pull towards it remains. Part of the significance of their journey is not just about what they do, but who they become as they grapple with the evil within.

This story has more than a single twist. There is actually a double resolution. Breathtaking a resolution though the resurrection is, it is not quite the last word. Jesus will return to this world and a time of reckoning will follow. Those who have responded to the invitation to follow him will be invited into a new order, a new heaven and a new earth, where each of these realms is somehow merged and a paradise, greater than the first and without its vulnerability, begins. It is a beautifully bookended story. Paradise, paradise lost, paradise restored – but magnified.

What 'Whole in Christ' Might Look Like: An Orthopathy Filter

If this is the narrative that shapes a Christian understanding of the world, what should we expect people who have been moulded by this story to look like? As with the early disciples, contemporary disciples of Christ are engaged in God's mission of transforming the world, while also steadily plodding along the equally complex inner journey of personal transformation as they strive to become a little more Christlike. But how will we know when that journey is heading in the right direction? What are the signs that we should look out for that speak of a genuine work of grace in the transformation of an individual?

Great care must be taken here. We are not to expect cookie-cutter replicas of each other. Indeed, if all Christians thought and looked and acted in exactly the same way, we should suspect that toxic faith is not far from the horizon, for the loss of individuality speaks more of control and suppression than it does of freedom and liberation. We should, however, assume that certain values and convictions are held in common. They might express themselves differently in the various contexts of life, but when you dig a little deeper, you would expect that essentially the same vision and values are driving the choices being made.

What, then, will someone who is being made whole in Christ look like? We will explore some clues from the overarching narrative of the Christian faith. It has led me to ten signs that are usually present when Jesus is genuinely at work in a person. I have tried to think outside of traditional categories, so while I don't doubt that someone in whom God is deeply at work will be prayerful and regular in church attendance and diligent in their study of the Scriptures, these are not the markers I have looked for. They are, after all, fairly superficial, and can mask a deeper and darker inner reality. I have therefore tried to link a genuine work of God to the intersection of orthopathy (right feeling and attitude towards something), orthodoxy (right thinking) and orthopraxy (right action).

The first, orthopathy, is the one most commonly overlooked, probably because it is the most difficult to define precisely. Orthopathy is often something that is sensed, rather than something that can be clearly articulated.[2] The older stay-at-home brother in Jesus' parable of the lost son (Luke 15:11–32) is a classic example of someone who could confidently claim orthodoxy for his beliefs and orthopraxy for his actions. But he was as lost as his wayward brother because at the level of orthopathy, all was amiss.

Likewise, Jesus warns that those who harbour anger and lust in their hearts are comparable to those who commit murder or adultery (Matt. 5:21,22,27,28). At the level of practice, this makes no sense, but when we recognize that nothing short of right motivation and feeling will do, we realize that Jesus was deeply serious about radically changing our inner being. Orthopathy matters.

August Turak helpfully discusses three levels of transformation in his book *The Business Secrets of the Trappist Monks*, and differentiates between a change in conditions, circumstances and being.[3] If, for example, you are very tired and take a holiday, you are likely to transform your condition. If you became very tired because your workplace was understaffed and underfunded, and you are able to employ additional staff and secure extra funds, you transform your circumstances. However, both of these transformations are essentially external. Real transformation involves a change of being. Turak draws from the Charles Dickens novel *A Christmas Carol* and suggests that it is like the conversion of Scrooge, who wakes up after his convicting Christmas Eve dreams a genuinely new man.

Here, then, are ten signs that I believe usually accompany deeper levels of change.

When Orthodoxy, Orthopraxy and Orthopathy Meet: Ten Signs

1. A sense of the sacred

Those who live in the Western world find themselves in a setting where secular assumptions are firmly enforced in political decision-making. The public sphere is secular, and any attempt to make it otherwise is firmly resisted. This is understandable given the regular abuse of power during the Christendom era, when the church was able to enforce its will on the wider society.

Those who believe in Jesus the Christ often face an enormous dilemma here. Societal forces affirm religious behaviour so long as it is confined to a religious ghetto – such as a building designed for sacred purposes. Problems arise when the beliefs affirmed in that space spill out into the public square. Without it being explicitly stated, we are encouraged to think dualistically. Church is the sphere where we should anticipate God encounters, while the rest of life should be God free.

Many Christians find this unproblematic. They might be able to claim an occasional breakthrough when they manage to enact a core Christian conviction in the workplace. Conceivably, they might go the extra mile in helping a colleague, or perhaps resist the urge to retaliate when treated poorly. Though these might be minor victories, they matter, and they represent a coming together of both belief and practice. However, most commonly they are viewed as pleasing exceptions, moments when faith was demonstrated in an otherwise God-abandoned space.

Less frequent is an ability to see through the smokescreen of dualism and to detect the fingerprints of God everywhere. While Jesus certainly spent some time in the temple and synagogues of his day, the bulk of his time was spent in unconsecrated places. When others looked and said, 'It's still four months until harvest', he saw a harvest already ripe for the taking (John 4:35).

When God deeply works inside a person, the sacred–secular divide disappears. All of life becomes holy, and every human encounter is sacred. That does not mean that religious jargon has to intrude into every discussion (for that is often a sign of toxic faith), but that openness to the Divine lies at the core of our being and is the default to which we perpetually return. Rather than 'whatever' being the cry of our life, when God is deeply at work in our being all of life becomes sacred. It is primarily an attitude of the heart – a triumph of orthopathy, albeit one consistent with orthodoxy that will work its way out into practice.

2. An affirmation of life

The Bible is clear that God created a good world and that, in spite of human rebellion, God's intention and plans for this planet are redemptive. Love is at the heart of creation, and therefore those impacted by the message of Jesus are filled with a gentle optimism that overflows into life. The affirmation of life begins in the realm of attitude and then overflows into the realm of action.

While some religious traditions extol the virtue of a life of self-denial and encourage an attitude of detachment towards the things of this world, a wholesome doctrine of creation will have none of this. The fruit of only one tree in the garden of Eden was forbidden. The remainder represented a paradise to be explored and enjoyed.

Jesus delighted in the flowers of the field, noting that even Solomon in all his glory was not as finely arrayed. He feasted with friends and turned water into wine at a wedding. He saw children as role models of genuine faith, and was probably impressed by their laughter, spontaneity and instinctive trust. He wept in the face of human loss, even though he knew he was to be the great death-defeater, and he restored the health of many. He delighted in proclaiming forgiveness from sin, even though his own life was placed in jeopardy each time he did so. There were times when he was angry, but it was always in the face of that which was exploitative, dehumanizing and cruel. He also had no time for pettiness, and radically reinterpreted the Sabbath laws so that they became a cause for celebration rather than an irritating burden. The portrait of Jesus found in Scripture is compelling. It is warmly life-affirming.

We should not confuse the affirmation of life with naivety. Christians are not committed to a Pollyanna-style optimism that refuses to face up to the complexity and brokenness of life. Rather, the conviction that all things will be reconciled in Christ provides the courage and confidence to be outward-facing and life-affirming. Christ is the hope of the world, and the presence of those who serve him is therefore required in the world. This is not a meaningless involvement, but one which fills each day with purpose and direction.

3. A bent towards creativity

Genesis 1:2 tells of the time when 'the earth was formless and empty, darkness was over the surface of the deep, and the Spirit of God was hovering over the waters'. It is into this bleak scenario that God speaks, and the creative word spoken sees all life spring into being. From nothingness, something of enormous beauty and complexity is born. The action speaks of a God whose creativity is without limits.

Humans are made in the image of God, and as image bearers are called to represent something of what God is like. They are God's icons, and while the representation can never be perfect or complete (especially in a post-fall world), it should not be misleading. Given that God delights in the variety of creation and has gifted us a world of endless hues and textures, it is unthinkable that we would allow our worship of God to become drab and predictable. That would be so unlike God. Likewise, our living should be boldly adventurous.

I remember his satirical tones. He was describing the dress code for the annual denominational gathering. It was the first I was to attend, and I had asked what to expect. He answered at length, but the shortened version was that if you were male, any clothing that was immediately forgettable was acceptable, while if you were female, you had to wear something that had been fashionable a decade (or two) ago. And he was right. While no uniform was prescribed, it was as if everyone present had conspired together to be as dull and unmemorable as possible. What was true of the clothing was matched by the decor and food. Nothing was badly wrong, but equally nothing was really right. It was a triumph of mediocrity, with blandness being the guiding virtue.

We could speculate at length why this describes all too many church events. While we do so, we should feel perplexed. This is not as it should be. When people tell me that they have given up on church attendance because they find services dull, I feel a similar sense of bewilderment, accompanied by a deep sadness. It does not have to be this way, and often it is not.

True, genuine creativity is hard work. But it flourishes in communities that affirm and encourage and are unafraid to experiment, and at times to fail. The church is called to be such a community – one where we invite each other to be more than we are on our own. This certainly often happens, and I have delighted in worship services

where every sense has been appealed to. I have been in churches where
drama and art and music flourish. I have heard messages where the
Bible springs into life as a result of deep engagement with and reflection upon its message. When this is accompanied by compassionate
involvement in society and thoughtful engagement with the issues of
the time, church is never dull. It is a risky venture of faith that sees
something birthed in the world's otherwise formless and empty places.
It is a triumph of the creativity that is intrinsic to our humanity.

4. Engagement with creation

It is hard to argue that you love the Creator if you want to have nothing to do with the resultant creation. The world is filled with the fingerprints of God, whose character and care can be seen in the design
of each leaf and flower, in both stormy days and clear, in butterflies
that delight and in mosquitoes that do not.

While engagement with creation reflects appreciation for its de-
signer, it is also an obedient response to the creation mandate entrusted to humanity to steward the world and to ensure its flourishing.
Names tell you so much. We are increasingly encouraged to care for
the *environment*. Christians view it a little differently. They believe in
care of *creation*. It makes a difference. If you believe that this is essentially an accidental universe without any inherent purpose other than
one which we chose to impose upon it, you need to rally the troops to
care for the *environment*. It doesn't come naturally – indeed, if this is
an accidental universe, nothing comes naturally.

Creation care flows from a different core conviction. God made
the world for a purpose and has called us to be responsible stewards
of creation so that it achieves its purpose. Christians look after the
world because God made it, and to be disrespectful towards God's
handiwork is to be disrespectful towards God.

While tending the earth, Christians also discover how wonderful
it is. In an increasingly synthetic world, Christ's followers are called
to be counter-cultural. They are distrustful of raising their children

on a diet of endless computer games at the expense of tree climbing or time at the beach. They recognize that standing before creation alerts one to the patterns and mysteries of life in a way that time at the shopping mall does not. While reading the Scriptures is richly rewarded, we should not underestimate the value of actively engaging in God's creation. Theologians have long spoken of the two books of God – the book of nature and the Bible. Both should be read and delighted in.

5. Open to multiple relationships

Acts 1:6–8 is fascinating reading. It starts disappointingly, as the disciples ask their last recorded question of Jesus, 'Lord, are you at this time going to restore the kingdom to Israel?' Their query reflects their priority. They had followed Jesus with a growing belief that he was the Messiah. When they thought 'Messiah', they thought of a leader who would rescue them from the oppressive rule of the Romans. They hoped for a king similar to David, who had led Israel to its greatest triumphs as a nation. In spite of spending three years with Jesus, their agenda is essentially parochial and self-centred. It is about their country, their people and their political and military well-being.

Was this, their final question before Jesus' ascension to his Father, a major disappointment to our Lord? We don't know, but the passage records that he immediately redirected their focus. Instead of thinking of a prominent role for Israel, they are to embark upon a mission of global significance. It is to change the world. Empowered by the Holy Spirit, they are to witness to Jesus in Jerusalem, Judea, Samaria and to the ends of the earth. The vision is expansive and inclusive. It triggers memories of Abram's original call, when he was informed that a result of his election would be that 'all peoples on earth will be blessed through you' (Gen. 12:3b). The tragedy of Abram's call was that it was quickly interpreted in terms of privilege rather than responsibility. The Jewish nation failed to be a light to the nations.

Jesus now calls his disciples back to the heartbeat of God. The concern is global.

When God deeply works inside a person or community there is an expansion of vision. It is never enough for us to be the sole recipients of God's grace. This good news must be communicated to others, and geographic and ethnic barriers must not be allowed to hinder its spread.

This conviction lies at the heart of Paul's liberating insight in Galatians 3:28 that in Christ 'there is neither Jew nor Gentile, neither slave nor free, nor is there male and female, for you are all one in Christ Jesus'. This sentiment, remarkable in Paul's time, is no less remarkable today. In a world that has allowed the superficial differences of race, class and gender to tear us apart, Christians operate from a different agenda. They allow these differences to enrich and enhance our appreciation of the diverse world that God has created. When God is at work, we are open to a range of relationships we might otherwise have closed our hearts to. The parochial subsides, and God's generous grace allows us to enjoy a range of relationships to which we might otherwise have been closed. All are enriched as a result.

6. Humble

Conversion to Christ begins with an act of humility. It starts when we realize that our own merits are insufficient to warrant our spending eternity with God. It requires us to recognize our need for forgiveness and to acknowledge our brokenness and sin. It involves bowing the knee to Jesus and accepting him as both Saviour and Lord. For the arrogant, this is simply too hard.

At the heart of original sin was the conviction that we had no need of God. The tempting promise of the tree of the knowledge of good and evil was that those who ate its fruit would know the difference between good and evil unaided. As our ancient ancestors bit into its fruit, they staked their independence from God. No longer would they need divine guidance to know how to live in their world – or so they thought. It was not to be.

The error was repeated at the tower of Babel. Humanity hoped to build a tower that would provide a route to heaven. Once it was built, God's help to reach this realm would be redundant. The human race believed it could reach heaven through its own ingenuity, the subtext of their effort reading, 'God, you are no longer required. Thanks for your help in the past, but you are now surplus to requirements.' Their arrogant confidence was unfounded, and a very different outcome resulted.

Conversion is the reversal of Eden and Babel. It is the point where we face our limitations and need, and acknowledge that God, rather than being the problem, is in the deepest sense the solution. It takes the humility of recognized failure to reach this point.

If conversion begins with the humility of acknowledged need, it continues in similar vein. Humility should not be confused with humiliation – for there is no humiliation in following Christ. But growth in the Christian faith requires an ongoing openness to becoming all that we are meant to be. God's plans for us are often more ambitious than our own. We are usually content to be a little better than most people, but Jesus sets the bar at perfection, calmly instructing in Matthew 5:48 that we are to 'Be perfect, therefore, as your heavenly Father is perfect'.

True, a Jewish understanding of perfection was different from our own. We equate perfection with being the best, whereas the Jews of Jesus' time thought that something that was fulfilling the purpose for which it was made was perfect. Using the logic of that time, a car that starts each time you turn the key and completes the intended journey in an acceptable time frame is perfect, even if it has numerous dents, tasteless decor and poor suspension. Cars are made to take you to places, and if they do that, they have achieved the purpose for which they were made, and can (in this way of thinking) be classed as perfect.

Each Christ-follower has the enormous privilege of knowing that God has a plan (or a range of possible plans) for their life. When we sign on as Christ-followers we are never at risk of being declared redundant. At the same time, fulfilling those plans requires an ongoing openness to change and growth. We will often be perplexed and dismayed at the extent of our brokenness. Like the apostle Paul, we will sometimes cry out, 'I do not understand what I do. For what I want to do I do not do, but what I hate I do' (Rom. 7:15). Sometimes, the struggle will be with what God wants to do through us. Even more often it will be about what God wants to do in us. Smug complacency is never an option. Even in our better moments, our motivation is often muddied and muddled, and it takes humility to stay close to the cross, gratefully receiving the forgiveness offered.

This is more than a theory. You quickly sense when someone is open to growth and change. They are willing to listen, to reflect and to learn. A gentle humility characterizes their being. Return to them in a year's time, and you will find they have progressed further in the life of faith.

7. Led, rather than leading

Hand-in-hand with humility is the awareness that Christ-followers are led, rather than leading. That does not mean that they do not hold leadership positions, but paradoxically, the higher the leadership position, the more important it is that the holder recognizes that they are not the one ultimately in charge and that Christian leadership must be held lightly. All Christian leaders should be led, and those who forget this often do great damage.

In practical terms, each Christian submits themselves to the teaching of Scripture. They try to understand its message by discussion and engagement with others on the journey. They try to remain open to the leading of the Spirit, and are willing to consult with other Christians as they try to discern if what they have heard is from the Spirit or is a product of their own imagination. Guidance is best when it is communal, and so we should be open to sharing our lives with each other, recognizing the risks and vulnerability that result from living transparently.

While our personal wishes and preferences are never irrelevant, they are not the sole determinant of the path we follow. Sometimes we make costly choices because we sense the good that might result and believe that this is the path that God has called us on. We are open to life being a purposeful adventure. The only guarantee is the faithfulness and goodness of God. Listening for the whispers of God is therefore part of the calling of each Christian disciple.

8. In a vocation rather than a job

One of the consequences of Adam and Eve's rebellion is that the work they previously found so enjoyable now becomes difficult and oppressive. In a post-fall world, our hard work only produces 'thorns and thistles', and modest though this harvest is, it comes 'by the sweat of your brow' (Gen. 3:17–19). The transformation of work from being a blessing to being a curse is one of the saddest results of our fall from grace. But our redemption in Christ includes the liberation of our work, for once we are in Christ, we are called to participate in his work of transforming the world.

It is interesting that in John 9:4 Jesus says, 'As long as it is day, we must do the works of him who sent me.' Note the 'we'. Jesus includes his disciples in the work he is called to do. This is then reinforced after his resurrection, when he commissions them to take his message to the furthest corners of the globe.[4] We should not think that this implies that those who are called to be missionaries and pastors have meaningful work while the remainder are trapped in dreary drudgery. The apostle Paul will have none of this, writing, 'Whatever you do, work at it with all your heart, as working for the Lord, not for human masters . . . It is the Lord Christ you are serving' (Col. 3:23–4).[5]

When we view our work as a way to glorify God, it transforms work from a task to a vocation. It is our call – the thing that we do in life that makes a difference. That does not mean that our work must be spectacular or unusual. I am deeply grateful when plumbers work for the glory of God, and likewise am appreciative of supermarket checkout staff who view their service as a way to honour God. True, that does not mean that Christian employees never make mistakes, or even that they are always the best at the job. Not everyone called by God has exactly the same ability, and some godly people have limited skill sets. However, regardless of aptitude, the desire to serve God through our labour makes a difference.

Those who serve Christ therefore do not think of their work as primarily being a way to fund their food and mortgage, but as a vehicle through which they will witness to God's love and care. William Placher has written, 'Central to many Christian interpretations of vocation is the idea that there is something – my vocation or calling – God has called me to do with my life, and my life has meaning and purpose at least in part because I am fulfilling my calling.'[6] While some might dismiss this as sounding too grand (I only serve coffee), when we dig a little deeper, those who serve Christ long to be used by him, and are as anxious to serve him in the marketplace as they are in sacred spaces. In reality, when we find our calling in the marketplace, it becomes a sacred place.[7]

9. Gracious

Probably the most distinctive Christian doctrine is that of grace – the conviction that our salvation is not the result of our own efforts, but because of Christ's death on our behalf on the cross. We bask in the unmerited favour of God because of Christ's sacrifice and mercy. We can claim no credit for ourselves. If we ask 'How can this be?' we must answer, 'Grace, grace and grace again.'

While we cannot earn grace, it permanently changes those who receive it. Or so you would think. Jesus sadly notes that this is not always the case, and in Matthew 18:21–35 tells the astonishing story of the unmerciful servant, who though he had been forgiven much, failed to show mercy to a fellow servant. The teaching point of the parable is clear and is expressed in verse 33: 'Shouldn't you have had mercy on your fellow servant just as I had on you?'

It is as well to be alerted that those who have received grace are not always as quick to confer it upon others. Jesus sees this as a grave miscalculation of the depth of our forgiveness, and warns that it can jeopardize that forgiveness (Matt. 18:32–5). Sometimes it is because we forget the magnitude of grace shown to us. The longer we serve Jesus, the greater the risk that we take our status as children of God for granted. When this happens, we can become smug and self-righteous, quick to spot the speck in the other's eye while oblivious to the plank in our own (Matt. 7:3–5). When grace seems a little less remarkable (because we forget the depth of our brokenness), we become shrill and unyielding, quick to judge and confident of our right to point the finger. When we stay close to the cross of Jesus, the risk of this diminishes. We remember the reality of our own story, and from deep inner gratitude are able to be gracious to others.

There is something winsome about people who have been shaped by grace. Their personal liberation sets them free to liberate others. It is wonderful to behold – faith at its transforming best.

10. Ever hopeful

I still remember his puzzled question. An immigrant from China, he was learning English in a class run by the church where I was the pastor at the time. Easter was approaching, and the group's leader had told the story of the crucifixion, noting that we would remember it that Friday on the day known as Good Friday. He came afterwards and asked me, 'How can you call it good? It was not good Friday, it was bad Friday. A very bad Friday.'

He had a point. How bizarre that we should describe crucifixion day as good. Of course, we know why we do. We no longer view the cross from the perspective of that bad Friday. We see it in the light of resurrection Sunday – and resurrection changes everything.

The journey to the cross had been filled with pessimism. The disciples had gloomily predicted that if Jesus persisted in his desire to return to Judea, great harm would befall him. Unable to dissuade him, Thomas summed up the resigned fatalism of the group in his words, 'Let us also go, that we may die with him' (John 11:16b). He would have drawn no pleasure in being able to say, on that terrible Friday, 'I told you so . . .'

But Easter Sunday was to dawn. That resurrection Sunday Jesus defeated sin, death and the devil – the terrible trio that had held humanity in bondage ever since their fall from grace.

Simply put, the resurrection is the death of pessimism. It is the permanent birth of hope. It is the reminder that God always has the last word – and God's word is resurrection. Thus Bad Friday morphs into Good Friday, for even the worst of news is transformed at the cross of Jesus.

Does this mean that Christians are always deliriously happy? No – we are not spared the struggles of everyday life. But at the deepest of levels, Christians harbour hope in their hearts. No matter how bleak the present moment, God will have the last word. We have every reason to hope.

Putting It Together

When we put these different pieces together we begin to glimpse how transforming and life-serving genuine faith can be. True, cynical readers might huff, 'That's a lovely portrait, but I don't know anyone like that.' There is a gap between who we have been called to be and who we are in reality.

View the portrait as invitational. It might not describe present reality, but it does depict the journey ahead. Imagine a church congregation filled with people who sense the sacred in the everyday, who are life-affirming, creative and creatively engaged with creation, who are open to a wide range of different and diverse people, who are humble and open to being led by God, viewing their work as a calling and a vocation, a place from which they will graciously and hopefully interact with God's world. Imagine such a world, and then allow the emerging picture to shape the decisions and direction of your life. This is an invitation to life-serving faith . . .

In Conversation with Rob Furlong

After serving as the senior pastor of Thornlie Church of Christ for twenty years, Rob Furlong recently accepted an appointment as the pastoral consultant for the Baptist Churches of Western Australia. Earlier in his ministry Rob experienced burnout, which became the focus of a research thesis he conducted at Vose Seminary.

Rob, this chapter has explored ways in which faith in Christ can liberate and transform, and has identified some of the signs that this is happening. But from your own experience, you know that the reverse can take place. Tell us a little about your experience with burnout.

Had you asked me how I was travelling in early 2006 I would have answered, 'Extremely well, thank you'! In addition to my regular pastoral duties I was running back-to-back groups for men struggling with sexual addiction, preaching and lecturing in India, carrying the brunt of the preaching load at church and had recently commenced my MA studies. I was feeling fulfilled in ministry and functioning well – or so I thought. However, throughout the year I was plagued with obsessive thoughts, and the more I fought these the worse they became. Everywhere I turned, whether at church or home, someone required something of me; this was especially so at church, where I was constantly faced with people running things by me for decisions that I felt they *could* and *should* be making themselves. I was not sleeping well and my personal life felt crowded – I had no time to process who I was or what was happening around me despite the fact that my spiritual disciplines were strongly in place.

This led to a very messy emotional, psychological and physical collapse later that year, which resulted in me having a six-month complete break from ministry. It was during that time that God began the slow task of rebuilding me in every aspect of my personhood and which included, as described in this book, a rediscovery of what it means to *affirm life* in all its vastness and wonder.

There was a bit of baggage from your upbringing, with your mother having a serious drinking problem. Has your faith helped you to re-frame the way in which you see that?

Most definitely! I was raised in the classic alcoholic family where everybody lives in denial that there is a problem, coupled with a lot of guilt, hostility, manipulation and emotional abuse. I have discovered in my faith journey that God confronts each of these behaviours directly, and he does so most often in the context of our closest relationships. Like it or not, and despite our best intentions, we *do* bring the baggage of our family of origin with us into these relationships.

Passages such as Romans 12:2 and Ephesians 4:17–32, along with the work of the Holy Spirit in my life, have enabled me to put off the poor ways of relating that I learned in my family and to develop much healthier ones. My faith has also informed the way I view my mum – to look beyond the alcoholic (which is still difficult to do at times!) and to see her as a broken person who also needs God's grace.

In your speaking ministry, you sometimes talk about having to come to terms with an anger problem. How has your faith helped you in this journey?

Anger in my family was always expressed inappropriately, usually in verbal and emotional abuse. I was aware that anger was a problem for me and was also taught at church that anger was an emotion that Christians should avoid at all costs. So for many years, when I felt angry, I simply supressed it, as good Christians do. But then it began to express itself in very unhealthy ways towards my children, as I had learned in my family of origin. As I began to confront this problem I saw that Scripture actually states that anger is a *valid* emotion (Eph. 4:26) to be felt – but it must be expressed appropriately (Eph. 4:29–32). Coupled with this was the fact that I knew I could not do this in my own strength. I was helped enormously by the statement of my principal in theological college, who had said that the key to growth as a Christian was not through the 'achieving will' (I can do this for God) but by the 'consenting will' (I willingly yield to the Holy Spirit producing his fruit in me). It was a slow process but God is *very* gracious, and I was also blessed with a loving and courageous wife in Karen.

Any advice for Christians who simply say, 'But I just don't feel whole'?

I like to remind people of who they are in Christ and point them to passages such as 1 Corinthians 6:11; 2 Corinthians 5:17; Galatians 2:20; 4:6,7; and Ephesians 2:8–10. At a practical level I have also found it helpful to share my story of God's work in my life and the changes he has brought about. This includes helping people understand that we are not perfect, that although we *are* whole in Christ we still carry our scars, but these are the very things that God uses in us in order to help others on their journey. After his encounter with God, Jacob walked with a limp for the rest of his life, but look at what God did through him! The good news is that God can do the same with us!

To Ponder and Discuss

1. Think about the three 'ortho's: orthodoxy, orthopraxy and orthopathy. Have you found the place where they merge together, or are your belief, practice and feelings at odds? If so, can you think of a path forward?
2. What might it mean for you to develop a sense of the sacred in places usually deemed secular?
3. Consider the two books of God – the Bible and nature. Are you reading both? How can your engagement with each deepen?
4. In practical terms, what might it mean for you to be 'led, rather than leading'?
5. How does the resurrection impact the way you approach life?

9

Life-Serving Faith: The Global Impact

I am fully persuaded that had Jesus Christ never walked the dusty paths of ancient Palestine, suffered, died, and risen from the dead, and never assembled around him a small group of disciples who spread out into the pagan world, the West would not have attained its high levels of civilization, giving it the many human benefits it enjoys today. One only needs to look to sectors of the world where Christianity has had little or no presence to see the remarkable differences – Alvin J. Schmidt.[1]

A Heartening Claim

In his intriguing book *Under the Influence*, Alvin Schmidt laments the 'pronounced paucity of information . . . regarding the influence and impact that Jesus Christ has had on the world for two thousand years'.[2] His book goes on to correct the deficit and its fifteen chapters argue that the birth of Christianity has directly resulted in:

- The sanctification of human life
- An elevation of sexual morality
- Freedom and dignity for women
- The birth of formalized charity
- The development of hospitals, health care and education
- Protection for workers and economic freedom
- The advancement of science
- The extension of liberty and justice to all

- The abolition of slavery
- Innovation in art, architecture, music and literature

The list is breathtaking, and while Schmidt is clearly accentuating the positives, his argument is compelling. While the Christian faith can turn toxic, in most instances it does not. The cumulative impact of tens of thousands of healthy church communities located around the world and throughout history should be overwhelmingly positive, and if Schmidt is right, what should be is matched by reality.

In this chapter we explore what local churches look like when they get things right. What are the signs of life-serving faith, and what are the likely results as it spreads and grows? Knowing what we are to aim at is one way to counter destructive alternatives, so a picture of the church as a genuinely alternative life-affirming community is important.

Snapshots from the Early Church

To build a picture of what the church should look like, it is helpful to look at its earliest expressions. While this is not as easy as we might imagine, there are some fairly clear lines that can be drawn.

Christianity succeeded in capturing the imagination of the Roman Empire, and in due course changed the world. This took place in spite of the early church facing obstacles which Michael Green describes as 'almost impossible to exaggerate'.[3] The disciples of Jesus were not well educated, they had little social influence, and they belonged to a conquered nation whose status had been downgraded to that of a second-class province on the Roman map.[4]

True, there were some factors that were helpful in the spread of Christianity. The *pax Romana* and the well-developed system of Roman roads made it possible for the early Christians to travel around the world in relative peace and safety. The widespread use of the Greek language ensured that their message was understood. In addition, Greek gods were seen as being cruel and despotic, so much so that Green has written, 'It was not that men became so depraved that they abandoned their gods, but rather that the gods became so depraved that they were abandoned by men.'[5] The world was open to looking for an alternative.

Beginning as a tiny offshoot of Judaism, by the end of the fourth century Christianity had morphed into the official religion of the Roman Empire. Much of this growth was the result of the passionate and sacrificial witness of many of the early Christians. Unafraid to proclaim the good news wherever they went, they had an enormous impact. They had an unyielding conviction that Jesus had been raised from the dead, and this gave them the confidence to face their own deaths, sometimes as a result of martyrdom.

Their message was liberating. Though they saw themselves as the completion of Judaism, they had a relaxed view of the law, and did not enforce dietary laws or regulations concerning circumcision. They were genuinely committed to each other, and were known for the depth of their love and concern for fellow believers. They came from all strata of society, although a disproportionate number were poor and struggling. Perhaps the poor, being on the fringes of society, had little to gain from clinging on to the status quo and were therefore more open to an alternative form of faith, or perhaps it was simply that Jesus spent more time with the poor and dispossessed than he did with the rich.

While Christianity started as a Jewish sect, it quickly broadened its horizons and included Gentiles as well. With this, the church's growth potential increased dramatically. The faith actively proselyt-ized and grew rapidly as a result. Periods of persecution were unable to stop this, leading to Tertullian's famous insight towards the end of the second century that 'the blood of the martyrs is the seed of the church'.[6]

In the Acts of the Apostles, Luke paints two summary portraits of the state of the church in its early stages (Acts 2:42–7; 4:32–7). It was a devoted community of believers who regularly met together for teaching, fellowship, breaking bread and prayer. They shared their possessions and willingly helped any who were in need. While they met in their homes, they retained their link with the temple. They experienced miracles. Their infectious joy and gratitude proved winsome, and each day saw more converts added to their ranks. Not that all was go and glow. Acts 5 records the disturbing deceit of Ananias and Sapphira (vv. 1–11), while Acts 6 informs us of the squabble around the distribution of food to widows (vv. 1–7). The growing opposition to the faith led to the first martyrdom in Acts 7, while Acts 8 tells of the persecution of the church in Jerusalem and the resultant scattering of the early believers. The church was in no monotonous routine, and they depended on God to help them meet the challenges of an ever-changing landscape.

What might this tell us about healthy faith? Seven factors stand out.

1. It was rooted in reality

You sense the struggle for faith and the struggle to uphold its standards. This was not an idyllic community – squabbles were never far from the surface. There were factions, personality clashes and disappointments.[7] For all that, there was a commitment to facing issues and to dealing with reality. Take Paul's willingness to confront Peter about the double standards he applied in his contact with Gentile believers. It is candidly spoken about in Galatians 2:11–14. Pressurized by the circumcision party, Peter had withdrawn his support from Gentile converts and had started to insist that they adopt Jewish customs. His capitulation affected others, so that even the warm-hearted and welcoming Barnabas began to treat Gentile converts as second-class Christians. Paul's record of the event is frank: 'But when Peter came to Antioch, I opposed him in public, because he was clearly wrong' (Gal. 2:11, GNT). There was no brushing of issues under the carpet, no pretence that everything was all right. Although it might seem strange to select the acknowledged conflict in the early church as a sign of its health, think of the toxicity of its alternative. When nothing is faced up to, nothing can change. It is soul-destroying to be part of a community where necessary conversations do not take place. Mark Strom has written of the void that exists in many organizations and suggests that 'This void is like a missing conversation'.[8] When we don't talk about the things that actually matter, great damage is done.

2. It was open to the other

The early church was outwardly focused. It was keen to expand its boundaries. It would have been easy for it to have become a small and irrelevant sect of Judaism. It was its willingness to reach out to Gentiles that ensured its long-term survival and impact. Not that this openness was easily attained. We have already mentioned the circumcision party that did its utmost to ensure that Gentile converts would be treated as second-class citizens. This was the acid test for the early church. If it had succumbed to this pressure (and Gal. 2:11–14 makes it clear that they almost did), it is unlikely that any church would exist today. In the quest for life-serving faith, we will invariably encounter those who wish to draw tight and narrow boundaries for the faith. Their default is to say 'no' and they often feel that excluding others is a sign of virtue. But Jesus trod on uncomfortable ground. There was nothing squeaky clean about his converts. His social circle raised the ire of the religious leaders of his day. We must notice the warning implicit in this. While I am not suggesting that there is no place for boundaries, the model of the early church suggests that we should open our hearts a little wider than they are naturally inclined to be.

3. It was developing and deepening in its understanding

A significant difference between the early church and the church today is that whereas we often feel that we have to fight for and defend the faith, they were in the process of discovering what the Christian faith meant. They carried with them numerous assumptions from their close link with Judaism, but as time went by, more and more of these were challenged and changed. Circumcision, Sabbath-keeping and dietary laws quickly diminished in importance. While the Hebrew Bible remained as a guide for faith and practice, it was interpreted in the light of the life, death, resurrection and anticipated return of Jesus. It took a while for the full implications of the gospel of grace to filter through, but as they did, one change after another took place. Instead of rules and regulations, they discovered freedom and the responsibility that must always accompany that precious gift. They were on the road to discover what orthodoxy meant for a new and fresh faith.

We are no longer in the early stages of doctrinal development and therefore should not expect the radical changes in understanding that they came to. For all that, we should guard against a static complacency that smugly assumes that we know all that is necessary. Healthy Christian communities regularly rethink the implications of faith in a changing landscape. It is not enough for us to ask what the Bible says. We must ask what it means and what principles lie behind the instructions given.

4. It was genuine

The ever-present threat of persecution ensured that the early believers had little time for posturing and pretence. They had staked their lives on the reality of Jesus and had everything to lose if their faith in him was misplaced. There is therefore no question that the vast majority were totally genuine in their faith and deeply committed to it. There really was no reason to embrace a tame or nominal version of Christianity. In our own day, people often lament the institutionalization of the church. It can seem corporate and contrived. While we should not be silly about this (any group meeting regularly over a period of time will institutionalize to some extent), we should be willing to go back to a grass-roots version of faith. Too often, our church communities are more about making Sunday happen than about genuinely following Jesus.

5. *It was courageous*

Many of the early Christians paid a significant price for following Jesus. While we tend to focus on those who were martyred, sometimes thrown to lions or burnt alive at the stake, many more were misplaced. They fled from the centres of persecution, effectively becoming refugees in the process. Undaunted, they continued to proclaim their faith, Acts 8:4 recording that 'Those who had been scattered preached the word wherever they went'. We should not underestimate the courage that it took to do this. While we might cite the saying 'Once bitten, twice shy', their thinking did not move in that direction. Courage is contagious and helps people to rise above their fears and insecurities. It helps us to rise above the petty and to see what really matters. The genuinely courageous are willing to lose what they presently have so that a better order can be birthed. Only the courageous are willing to embark upon real change, and their example often inspires others to follow suit.

6. *It was compassionate*

The earliest snapshots of the church portray a community where, to cite Acts 4:32, 'All the believers were one in heart and mind. No one claimed that any of their possessions was their own, but they shared everything they had'. The result is recorded in verse 34: 'there were no needy persons among them'. All were taken care of as a result of the compassion of their fellow Christians. They valued qualities such as gentleness (Phil. 4:5) and committed themselves to focusing on what was true, noble, right, pure, lovely, admirable, excellent or praiseworthy (Phil. 4:8). People flourish within these boundaries, and at a time when cynicism and scepticism are the new norm, we have much to learn from this more generous and hopeful era.

7. *It was a genuine alternative*

In a highly stratified world where slaves and masters had nothing to do with each other and lived radically different lives, Christianity offered an alternative vision of human relationships. Paul encouraged that the runaway slave Onesimus be viewed 'no longer as a slave, but . . . as a dear brother' (Phlm. 1:16). The old divides melted away in the light of the new allegiance to Jesus. We might have become accustomed to the teaching of Galatians 3:28, but try to hear its words with first-century ears: 'There is neither Jew nor Gentile, neither slave nor free, nor is there male and female, for you are all one in Christ Jesus.' This was revolutionary for its time – actually, it is still revolutionary today.

There are of course other things we could say about the early church. Clearly it was a God-fearing community. It was spiritually empowered and open to the leading of God's Spirit. It stood at a unique time in history. It was fallen and made many mistakes. But imagine the impact if we were to build communities of faith that emulated their strengths . . . if we, rooted in reality, were open to the other, growing and deepening in our understanding of the faith, and added to this a genuine, courageous, compassionate and fresh, alternative vision of life. We might reshape the world for the better.

Contemporary Options

If the early church provides some clues as to what we should strive for, we can also look at some contemporary examples for guidance. In many ways it is easier to note what to avoid. Here are ten signs that you might be entering abusive church territory:

1. It's all about the leader
2. It operates independently and there is no appropriate oversight
3. Unrealistic promises are made

4. The end justifies the means, and those hurt along the way are viewed as necessary casualties of a worthier cause
5. Those who leave are shunned
6. Theology is reactionary and recited in a mindless, parrot-like fashion
7. Too much information is requested from members, be it how much they earn, who they have slept with, or who they plan to leave their money to
8. Outsiders are the enemy
9. Decisions cannot be questioned
10. Everyone in power is related to the leader, or all other 'leaders' are clearly pawns of the real leader

Enough of the negatives. Here are seven signs that you are in life-serving territory:

1. God matters

While this might sound obvious, when churches forget that they exist for the glory of God, other motivations find their way onto the agenda. They are rarely healthy. There are many indicators that suggest whether or not God matters to a particular church congregation. When God is central to the church's agenda, worship is real, the Scriptures are read and relevantly applied, and prayer is heartfelt. Spiritual disciplines are usually part of the church's life, though we should not be too quick to judge if one or two are missing. The quest is not for a flawless community but for an authentic one, where people are open to growth and look to God for guidance and strength. There are many ways in which genuineness can be expressed, and we should not confuse it with heartiness or the volume of the music nor the length of the service. Though some will find this statement frustratingly vague, you can sense when you are in a church where God matters to the people. If you don't sense it, be wary.

2. People matter, and relationships are real

You pick this up very quickly. Usually the surest sign is how long people remain behind after the worship service ends. When the premises are quickly vacated, it probably means that there is little depth in the relationships between people. Of course, if it is because small groups are going off to picnic or lunch together, that is a different matter. There needs to be a genuine communal life. The instruction of Romans 12:15 is crisp, clear and pertinent: 'Rejoice with those who rejoice; mourn with those who mourn.' It is impossible to do that unless we know something of the lives of the people we worship with. Not that we should impatiently dismiss a local church where deeper relationships are absent. Often it takes only a small handful of people who are willing to be authentic and transparent to change the dynamics of a church. There is no reason why you shouldn't be one of them.

3. Purpose and vision are evident

We all have a need for our lives to matter. I have been a pastor for long enough to know how devastating it is when a person approaches the end of their life, looks back, and concludes that very little of what they did was of any significance. Undoubtedly the greatest cause of that pain is when relationships have failed and the person faces their death with a sense that it is unlikely to really matter to anyone. Not too far behind that is a sense that nothing they did was of any real value. It is a reminder that churches should not waste people's time. Too often, our concern is to make Sunday happen rather than to make a difference. A quick test of a healthy church is if it has a clear sense of purpose and vision. I don't mean exaggerated, over-the-top claims that this local church is going to change the world. Making a bit of a difference in its own setting is an adequate start. To do that, we need to look out for churches that know what they are trying to do and which systematically set about trying to do it. We should ask if the tasks the church attempts to recruit people for are worthy of their time and effort, and if they are likely to lead to tangible results.

He had come to the church office to make a generous donation. 'It is nothing in comparison to the difference you made to Dad's life,' he said. 'We had been so worried about him. We live so far away, and work made it impossible to spend much time with him. We could see he was losing all interest in life. And then he found this place. I don't know what you did, but suddenly his world changed. We can never thank you enough.' The funeral had taken place a few weeks before, and I had often thought of Peter during that time.[9] He had simply arrived at church one day, and when I discovered he lived close by, I suggested that he pop into the office for a chat – which he did. He came unannounced, and it proved to be providential. There was a minor crisis on the go. We ran a feeding scheme at a school in a squatter community about a twenty-minute drive away. The small team of helpers had the food ready, but found themselves without transport when the driver's car wouldn't start. Mine was away for repairs, and we wondered what to do. For the 100 children fed by this scheme, this was likely to be their only nutritious meal for the day, and it looked as though we would not be able to get it to them. But Peter had just walked through the door, and hearing what had happened, immediately said that he would drive the team out. It ensured those children were fed that day, but it also changed Peter's life. He became the regular driver for the team – never missing a shift until his death. A few months after he started, God became real to him. His life gained focus and direction.

Here was a local church that had found a few meaningful things they could do well. They were genuinely helpful to the community, but they also made a difference in the lives of the church members who ran them. They weren't just filling people's time. They were building memories and shaping stories.

4. The church is good news in the way it does things and in its approach to life and society

A key indicator is whether the church has an outward or an inward focus. Inwardly focused churches usually become increasingly small-minded and are bothered by things that don't matter greatly. By contrast, an outward focus ensures a largeness of vision. This might sound a little nebulous, but perhaps an example will help.

In the early days of the outbreak of AIDS, churches could be divided into three categories by their response. There were those who adopted the wagging finger, immediately pontificating that those with lax sexual morals shouldn't lament the inevitable consequences. It was a less than helpful response, and caused both deep hurt and resentment. Churches which responded in this manner turned their backs on people when they were most needed and when their help was most likely to be sought. It was rejecting people at the point of their need, and it is impossible to reconcile these actions with the incarnational model of Jesus.

The majority of churches adopted the ostrich approach. They carried on as usual, but made no special effort to help those directly or indirectly impacted by AIDS. They thought that this approach did no harm, but it quietly sent a message to the world that when a real need arose, the church was essentially irrelevant. Again, this was less than helpful and a sub-Christian response. You cannot imagine Jesus adopting a stance of detached indifference.

Fortunately there were churches which realized that the call to care comes most loudly when life is at its messiest and most broken. At a time when those with AIDS were being shunned by those fearful of contamination,[10] they opened their hearts, lives and purses and gave time, empathy and treasure. They embodied the good news and lit candles of hope that remain alight to this day.

Moving away from this particular example, the three categories remain valid and are the ones we should assess. We should avoid churches that delight in pointing the accusing finger, just as we should be wary of churches that remain calmly and irrelevantly detached from the concerns of the day. An active embrace of life and its challenges characterizes churches that make a God-honouring difference.

5. The past is honoured, the present is embraced, and there is openness to the future

A toxic trap is either to be dismissive of the past, or to make the opposite error and be entrapped by it. In Hebrews 11 we are reminded of the great cloud of witnesses who attempted to serve God before Jesus' birth. Their example is cited to encourage us in our present efforts. Often they served God at great cost and at personal peril. 'Remember' is a key biblical word, and we should be cautious of the chronological snobbery of our age that assumes that only that which is current is of any real value. We have much to learn from the past and should honour it. However, we are called to live in our own time and era, and are responsible for the way in which we respond to its challenges. Healthy churches are alert to the needs of the present time, and refuse to be trapped in a time warp where only that which is old and fading can be considered to be of worth. Even while rooted in the present, we must be open to the challenges of the future. Each generation must pass the baton on to the next. We should ask if our actions in the present will make it a little easier for a later generation to serve Christ faithfully. The dance between past, present and future is not easy, and can become destructive. Healthy churches are aware of the tension and find a way to say 'yes' to each.

6. Generosity is evident

Faith in Christ gives a quiet confidence for the future. Churches know that God is no one's debtor and are willing to use their resources for the wider good. Many churches have significant buildings, and healthy churches think of ways to strengthen their community through good stewardship of what they have. Generosity refers not only to the use of financial resources. Healthy church communities are generous with their time and expertise. They are also generous in their judgements, willing to believe the best of others, rather than to assume the worst. They see each person in the community as made in the image of God, and while conscious of the impact of the fall, are hopeful that each can come to a transforming relationship with God. Their stance is therefore warm and invitational, for they know that they are Christ's representatives in their area.

7. The church matters to the community

Here's a true story: I had been invited to preach at a church that will remain nameless. It was over twenty years ago, long before mobile phones were a necessary part of existence – which in this instance proved problematic, because I lost my way. I had preached at the church before, but roadworks had seen a change in the road layout and my map was out of date. With the service start time drawing ever closer, I stopped at a local cafe to ask for directions. They were unable to help, and were equally unwilling to oblige when I asked if I could use their phone. Fortunately a fellow shopper took pity on me and said I could use his phone and, as he lived just a few blocks away, I could follow him back to his home, which I did. As I climbed out of the car I looked around, and to my delighted surprise, spotted that the church was directly across the road. I told the man that this was the church I was looking for, and his jaw dropped in surprise. 'Good gracious me!' he said. 'I have lived here for over a decade, and I have never noticed there was a church there before.' Clearly my new acquaintance was less than observant, but he didn't seem to be joking. Here was a church that didn't disturb the neighbours, but it was also monumentally irrelevant. This example might be extreme, but while most would notice if they had a church on their street, it is not uncommon for them to have never entered its doors. The reasons are many and are not always the fault of the local church; but healthy local churches make some difference to their community. A question to ask is, 'If we closed the doors of this church, would the local community feel the loss and would they care?'

There are many other signs to look out for. Churches that practise genuine hospitality can make an enormous difference. I have seen how effective this is in helping new immigrants settle. Hebrews 13:2 reminds us that those who practise hospitality might entertain angels without being aware of it, while Matthew 25:31–46 informs us that in welcoming the stranger, we might well be welcoming the unrecognized Christ. This conviction is part of the essence of our faith, and in an increasingly depersonalized world, can be transformative.

Although the contribution of any one local church might seem to be modest, we should not underestimate the cumulative effect of congregations around the world engaging in relevant grass-roots activities. There are many metaphors for the church, but one of the most striking is that of the body of Christ. When each local church sees itself as the eyes, hands, feet and voice of Jesus, and commits to being an authentic representation of Christ in its own time and setting, the overall global impact is enormous. The church has persistently changed the course of history. There is no reason why it should not continue to do so in the future.

In Conversation with Phillip Nash

Phillip Nash is the Head of School of a Pelita Harapan School in Jakarta, Indonesia, and co-ordinator of five of these schools established over the past twenty years by an Indonesian charitable foundation. These exclusive private schools intentionally use much of their surplus to establish schools in some of the neediest areas of Indonesia, where the foundation then provides education at a cost affordable to the poorest.

Phillip, what brought a New Zealander like you to Indonesia?

I have been involved in Christian schools in Australia and New Zealand for over twenty-five years and had a friend who worked here in Jakarta. At a point of change in my life, I was offered the chance to come here and get involved in an amazing vision. I have always enjoyed the mission opportunity Christian schools offer to their students and families, but this school offers the chance to impact thousands of students and families across Indonesia, the largest Muslim nation in the world.

Your school provides a fairly exclusive education from a Christian perspective. What difference do you hope to make in the life of your graduates?

Our schools exist to equip children from wealthy Indonesian families with a high-quality education taught from a biblical perspective and in an atmosphere of Christian community. Our mission statement is: 'Proclaiming the pre-eminence of Christ and engaging in the redemptive restoration of all things in him through holistic education.' Only about 50 per cent of our students come from Christian homes, so we are intentional about ensuring the gospel is preached and Christian students are discipled. Our approach to education sees discipleship as far broader than just a spiritual-development exercise but as a holistic one in which academic subjects and skills are part of equipping a young person to be an effective follower of Christ. We want our graduates to use the privileged position they have in Indonesian society as a platform for spreading the gospel in its fullness into every part of Indonesian society.

The school's financial model is a little different from most. Why and what are you hoping to achieve?

Our foundation has a three-fold vision for Christian schooling in Indonesia: schools for the upper, middle and lower socio-economic strata of Indonesia. We, and the middle-tier schools, are expected to contribute to the foundation's work in building and operating quality schools in the poorest parts of Indonesia to give the children there a real opportunity in life. A quality education can make a temporal difference in anyone's life; a Christian quality education can make an eternal difference. There are now seventeen such schools serving over seven thousand students across Indonesia.

What we are doing is community development at its most real. Not temporary relief of the poor, but the opportunity for poor children to move out of their poverty and discover a purpose and meaning to life that their poverty keeps them from. This is the gospel in its most practical expression.

What constructive contribution do you see the church making in Indonesia?

Some of the traditional Indonesian churches are trapped in a time warp where change is resisted and they are becoming increasingly irrelevant. Some of the more recently established churches, however, are really trying to engage with local and national communities in life-changing ways. Sadly, the West's prosperity gospel is rife here as it often is in poor communities. Churches like the Jakarta International Christian Fellowship run significant programmes reaching out in gospel-centred and practical ways to orphanages, supporting evangelistic ministries, and undertaking emergency and crisis relief, community development, and so on. Churches that seek to be Christ-centred all seem to engage in practical outreach to the community rather than just focusing on themselves.

To Ponder and Discuss

1. Reflect on the seven characteristics of the early church listed in the chapter (rooted in reality; open to others; developing and deepening in its understanding; genuine; courageous; compassionate; a genuine alternative). Would you describe your local church in similar terms? If not, what can be done to make these descriptions true for it?

2. Reread the ten warning signs that a local church might be entering abusive territory. Are any a risk in your setting? If so, how should you respond? If not, how can you ensure it stays that way?

3. Consider the three common responses given by local churches in times of crisis: the wagging finger, the ostrich approach or open-hearted engagement. Which is the default drive of your local church and why do you say this? Does it need to change? If not, how can you preserve its healthy instinct?

4. If you asked each person in your local church if it most honours the past, the present or the future, which answer would be given most frequently? Have you found the healthy point of intersection?

5. If you asked your community what difference your local church makes, what do you think the answer would be?

10

Theology Matters: The Case for a Core Conviction

Some Background

'What we believe matters.' It sounds like such a simple statement. But how do we arrive at our beliefs? Let's face it, although we would sometimes like to fool ourselves to the contrary, all Christians do not believe exactly the same thing. While most commonly the differences are minor and reflect a robust faith that does not have to find security in everyone parroting exactly the same thing, at other times the differences are substantial and reflect not just a different version of faith, but a significantly different vision for it.

Let us return to our key question. How do we arrive at our beliefs? Some would naively answer, 'That's easy. The Bible determines our belief system.' But it is not that simple. After all, the early Christians had some clear doctrinal views before the Bible was finalized and available in its current form. Simply stated, the church predates the Bible. True, the Bible Jesus knew was available to them, but the Christian faith has moved a long way from the Jewish faith, largely because we usually read the Old Testament (or the Hebrew Bible) with a Christological lens. In other words, we interpret what we read in the Old Testament in the light of the life, death, resurrection and future return of Jesus. When you read with a lens, it impacts what you see and where you place your emphasis.

So how do we arrive at our beliefs? It is a question of theological method. Some might sigh at this statement, and fear that this book is drawing towards a complicated ending. But I consider this chapter to perhaps be the most relevant in this book. Even if the material in the second half of this chapter is a little more complex, I encourage you to persevere. The concepts are important.

A few years ago I was asked to present a paper on why I consider theological method to be so important.[1] I have reproduced it below, but have edited what I said to make the material more accessible. When we take on board the underlying principles, it will be a little clearer why our choice of the way we do theology has such a significant impact on what we finally believe. And what we believe eventually determines if we embrace a life-serving or toxic version of faith.

Why This Topic?

In the wing of Christianity in which I find myself, broadly dubbed evangelicalism, theological inquiry is often seen as the death of spiritual passion or, at best, a dangerous enterprise. If I were to say that my theological passion revolved around establishing the trustworthiness of Scripture, or that it centred on the significance of the cross, focused on the nature of conversion or helped motivate the church towards greater activity in serving God, my concerns would be deemed appropriate and helpful.[2] But when I make the embarrassing confession that my theological passion focuses on the area of theological method, mild interest rapidly changes to an all-too-obvious attempt to change the topic. Why would anyone be passionate about theological method?

A reluctance to engage with questions of theological method may be more prevalent in evangelical circles than in others, with Grenz and Franke maintaining that while 'theologians in mainline theological circles have been in need of a reminder that theology involves more than simply reflecting on method . . . [e]vangelical theologians have . . . given little attention to methodological concerns'.[3] So why did I depart from this norm? Let me explain my motivation by indulging in some personal reflections.

I did not have the privilege of growing up in a committed Christian home, and most certainly not one characterized by evangelical convictions. However, the practice of my parents, in keeping with the general practice of the South Africa of the 1960s, was to send their children to the local Sunday school until such time as they were confirmed by the church. Having been suitably Christianized we were then to be released from the burden of church attendance.

My two sisters glided through the system effortlessly, but my progress stalled when the newly appointed minister of our local Congregational church announced that he was discontinuing the annual confirmation service. In his previous church he had confirmed 120 young people, of whom only two ever returned to the church. Disillusioned by the system he imposed a moratorium. Uncertain how to navigate this ecclesiastical crisis, my mother instructed me to keep attending until the pastor came to his senses – which he didn't. During this impasse, renewal came to the congregation, and I came to faith.

Shortly afterwards my parents' marriage terminated, and as part of the divorce settlement we moved to alternative accommodation a few suburbs away. My mother did not drive, and as the Congregational church was no longer local or within walking distance, I had no choice but to nurture my faith in a different church community. Though the return trip required trudging up an excessively steep hill, Calvary Baptist Church[4] met the 'within walking distance' requirement, and so it was that I became a Baptist, not from strong doctrinal convictions, but from an absence of choice – not necessarily the best motivation for someone who in time was to become the principal of a Baptist theological college.

Calvary Baptist Church epitomized both the best and the worst of evangelical faith. It was a new family – more truly home than my own home – and I embraced all that it stood for with fervour and zeal. The friendship, kindness and acceptance that I experienced in that congregation were so superior to anything I had previously experienced that it was only with the deepest reluctance that I critiqued any of its practices. But some of them mystified me. There was its staunch opposition to the drinking of any alcohol. When I pointed to Jesus' miracle of turning water into wine as a counter to the church's teetotal stance (John 2:1–11), it was explained to me that actually Jesus turned water into non-alcoholic grape juice, and that this was the reason the master of the banquet declared it superior to the wine previously supplied. The medicinal value of non-alcoholic grape juice was seen as further proved by Paul's advice to Timothy to take a little wine for the good of his stomach (1 Tim. 5:23) – clearly something that would not be achieved if actual alcohol was consumed. I wasn't convinced, but compliance with the stance was a negligible price for the return of belonging to such a family.

More troubling was the church's stance on women in leadership. Paul's statements that women should learn in quiet and full submission and that no woman should teach a man seemed at best unfair (1 Tim. 2:11–14). I was acutely conscious of my own mother's struggle to hold our family together. Against the odds she managed to ensure that I and my two sisters received a tertiary education. I might have been male, but I knew that I had much to learn from her. Again, my growing knowledge of Scripture saw me counter the argument. I tried Galatians 3:28 – that in Christ there is neither male nor female – but was assured that all that meant was that both men and women could become Christians. I was unconvinced, but had no doubt that I was male, and was therefore prepared to suppress my dubiousness as none of it applied to me. It was easy to forget my concerns, as Calvary Baptist was filled with women who seemed perfectly content to follow an exclusively male leadership.

Perhaps the most traumatic moment was when a close friend of mine, the first of my friends to have become a Christian at Calvary Baptist, announced that he was gay. I was stunned, as were all in our circle. As far as we were concerned, this was a realm that simply did not exist. We did our best and whisked Paul[5] to one healing meeting after another. It was all to no avail. A few months later he announced that he was leaving the church and would be moving in with a man from the choir – news which we found equally appalling. This was a line too far for us. We did not know what to do, but our pastor, presumably having heard some rumours, departed from his usual kindly demeanour and launched into a diatribe against homosexuals in the middle of a sermon on a completely unrelated topic. The message was clear: those who wandered to Sodom would have to do so alone. Our group parted company with Paul, reassuring ourselves that he would return when he saw the folly of his ways. I never saw him again, hearing only that he had attempted to contact me shortly before his death of an AIDS-related disease. I have often wondered what we would have said to each other had his efforts been successful. I continue to feel both outraged and ashamed that I was part of a system that so ruthlessly turned its back on someone at a time of such great insecurity and need. It has left me with more than a few troubling questions.

One further question unearthed during my time at Calvary Baptist was of the relevance, or otherwise, of the Christian faith to the political status quo. It was here that the church was at its most disunited. I grew up in apartheid South Africa, and the trauma of that time was the backdrop to our theological musing. The majority focused on Romans 13 and its call to obey the government. They were opposed by the Amos and Isaiah 58 faction. I had no doubt where my loyalty lay. Everything within me resonated with Isaiah's plea that we release the chains of injustice and set the oppressed free.

My convictions were rooted in my exposure to the narratives of some black South Africans. While Calvary Baptist, like far too many South African Baptist churches in that troubled era, was largely uncritical of the political status quo, it contained some surprising – indeed heroic – pockets of dissent. Some returned medical missionaries involved in training black medical students in the local university introduced me to some of their students. The apartheid system was designed to make such encounters near impossible, but in this instance it failed. The friendships formed were transforming. While I had not yet been exposed to Anton Boisen's plea that theological students 'learn to read human documents as well as books', I intuitively grasped its validity.[6] The stories of my friends were overwhelming and convicting. Never, never, never again was I able to listen to a sermon from Romans 13 that suggested that unquestioning obedience to the political status quo was required of all Christians[7] without a simultaneous rise in blood pressure and a sweeping sadness that the biblical text could be perverted into a text of terror.[8]

Throughout these experiences I was developing a niggling unease as to the way theological positions were being reached. Many churches in South Africa used the Bible to justify apartheid, while others around the world condemned apartheid as a heresy.[9] I started to wonder if in addition to Scripture there were unacknowledged factors that helped steer theological conclusions, and speculated about the role of cultural, sub-cultural and contextual drivers. It was around this time that I was exposed to what is often misleadingly referred to as the Wesleyan Quadrilateral, which proposes that the four sources for theological construction are Scripture, tradition, reason and experience.[10] It caught my imagination, and I even went so far as to present an embarrassingly amateurish paper on the topic at a student conference.[11] It was thus that my theological passion, a persistent questioning of the method by which we arrive at theological conclusions, was birthed.

Discovering Grenz

In pursuing this passion I discovered Stanley Grenz's work on theological method. It struck me as deeply significant.[12] I have concluded that, with some minor modifications, his method[13] has the potential to genuinely revision evangelical theology. In his various works a theological method that has the potential to be faithful, hopeful and loving emerges.[14] I say 'potential' because my study of Grenz led me to the conclusion that he did not fully unpack the possibilities inherent in his method, largely because he did not critique the limitations in his approach carefully enough.

Grenz proposes a model for evangelical theological construction that utilizes Scripture, tradition and culture as the sources for theology, and the Trinity, community and eschatology as its focal motifs. He supplements these with the belief that the Spirit guides the church as it communally attempts to discern truth in changing contexts. Grenz believes that his method moves beyond foundationalism as it appeals to a trio of interacting, conversing sources that are guided by three related motifs, rather than to the single source of Scripture.[15]

Suggesting Scripture as a source for theological construction is something of a non-negotiable for any theological method that wishes to be considered evangelical.[16] For evangelical method, the debate is more over seeing Scripture as *a* source or *the* source for theological conclusions, with the latter serving as the default drive. There is therefore nothing inherently novel in Grenz's suggestion that Scripture serve as theology's 'norming norm'.[17] Of greater interest are the shifts in emphasis proposed by Grenz.

Grenz argues that postfundamentalist evangelical theology has continued to adopt a propositionalist approach, with the theological task being conceived as the discovery and articulation of the one doctrinal system embedded in the Bible.[18] We should not accept Grenz's analysis uncritically, as he is a little one-sided in his presentation of propositionalist approaches.[19] Rather than follow a propositional programme, Grenz suggests that theology should be conceived as the 'reflection on the faith commitment of the believing community'.[20] He suggests that the Bible's authority derives from it being 'the source for the symbols, stories, teachings and doctrines that form the cognitive framework for the worldview of the believing community'.[21]

Second, he believes that many evangelicals 'take loyalty to the Bible to heights not intended by the Reformers and not in keeping with the broader trajectory of the evangelical movement'.[22] He argues that such loyalty is misguided and unnecessary. The Bible's status as the foundational text of the faith community guarantees its place of importance in the theological enterprise. Grenz's approach at this point is essentially pragmatic and functional. If theology is the reflection on the faith commitment of the believing community, it is a reflection that cannot begin without an understanding of the 'book of the community'.[23]

From a traditional evangelical perspective, this is provocative. Evangelicals assign a place of prominence to the Bible out of a conviction that its message is the truth and its revelation the sole surety for statements made about the nature and character of God.[24] The constituting role of the Bible in the life of the church is seen as of secondary importance to the claim that it is an accurate and authoritative revelation of the character, will and actions of God. Grenz's stance seems a short step from relegating the Bible to a text of historical (but not authoritative) importance. In addition, his argument that the Bible's role as the repository of the original kerygma of the faith community guarantees it a role of ongoing importance is not self-evidently true. Belief systems can change and evolve, and most would not consider a stance definitive simply because it was the one originally adopted.

A third aspect of Grenz's proposal on Scripture, and one which reflects something of the heartbeat of his concern, is expressed in his approving discussion of the Pietists. He notes, 'For the Pietists, talk about the truth claims of the Bible was less important than the fact that "truth claims" – that the Scriptures lay hold of the life of the reader and call that life into divine service.'[25] While probably a false dichotomy, it leads to the next stage of Grenz's thinking about Scripture.[26] Grenz stresses that the meaning and impact of Scripture is pneumatologically mediated. He laments that the theological method of most Protestant theologians separates its discussion of the Bible from its discussion on pneumatology – which is the study of the work of the Holy Spirit.[27]

In practical terms, Grenz calls evangelicals to pay as much attention to the doctrine of illumination as they do to inspiration. By placing the emphasis on the inspiration of Scripture, a static view of Scripture can dominate. Arguments revolve around the once-for-all divinely given message of Scripture, rather than around the need to listen to the ongoing voice of the Spirit speaking through Scripture (illumination).

This focus on illumination shifts the subject–object locus. So long as we have an inspired text to study, the theologian can approach Scripture as an objective text whose message can be interpreted and explained. If, however, the focus shifts to Scripture as a Spirit-illuminated text dynamically interacting with the life of the community, the static 'given' of the text is replaced by uncertainty, ambiguity and the subjectivity of a required response.

Grenz's pneumatologically mediated approach to Scripture has led to concerns being expressed. A major refrain is that the approach is subjective and undermines the concept of the authority of Scripture by taking the locus of authority from the text and placing it within the contextualized, Spirit-guided community of faith. Consequently, some evangelicals have been dismissive of Grenz's proposal, Carson complaining, 'I cannot see how Grenz's approach to Scripture can be called "evangelical" in any useful sense.'[28]

Grenz's second source for theology is tradition. In exploring tradition as a theological source which serves as theology's hermeneutical trajectory, Grenz attempts to answer the question of how the insights gained from the Spirit's guidance and leading of the church over the last two thousand years can be utilized in the process of theological reflection.[29] In suggesting that tradition serves as a hermeneutical trajectory, pointing towards the eschatological future of the church on the basis of insights from the past, and in turn being critiqued on the basis of the eschatological vision, he hopes to overcome static views of tradition that have led to an impasse between opposing groups, as each tries to justify their tradition as the valid one.

Grenz's revisioned theology is intended to win over two audiences. On the one hand, it is *evangelical* theology that he revisions, and his hope is to draw traditional evangelicals to a broader vision of the movement. On the other hand, he writes for the *postmodern* context, and seeks to develop a theology that is true to its evangelical roots but which is a respected player in the postmodern arena. For neither of these audiences is tradition an obvious choice as a source for theology.

However the roots of evangelicalism are traced, it is never less than a movement supportive of the Reformers' cry of *sola scriptura*. Indeed, the perceived use of tradition at the expense of the Scriptures was a key factor in the Protestant Reformation.[30] In suggesting tradition as a source for theology Grenz therefore has to indicate how to move beyond the hermeneutics of suspicion from which evangelicals usually operate when appeals to tradition are made in theological construction.

Neither is the choice of tradition self-evident for a postmodern audience. Wentzel Van Huyssteen accurately summarizes a key postmodern concern about the use of tradition when he writes, 'By seeking to disturb any easy relationship with our past by arguing that our assertion of continuity is itself an invention of our need to control the destiny of our culture and society, a sceptical form of the postmodern critique of continuity thus calls into question the very possibility of tradition.'[31]

While aware of these reservations, Grenz provides four persuasive reasons for using tradition as a theological source:

1. Past doctrinal statements and theological models are instructive for the present theological quest and help to avoid the pitfalls from the past.
2. Traditions serve as a reference point.
3. Some doctrinal formulations have withstood the test of time.
4. As a second-order task, theology is undertaken by theologians who are themselves members of a faith community which spans the centuries.[32]

While Grenz's case for appropriating tradition as a conversation partner with Scripture and culture is sensible, he glosses over the problems inherent in the approach. His claim that the believing community will be guided by the Spirit to discern which aspects of tradition to embrace flies in the face of the very history of the church that Grenz wishes to uphold. Even a cursory glance through church history establishes the wide range of conflicting answers that have been adopted by different segments of the faith community. Grenz is silent on how this impasse is to be overcome, other than to note the helpfulness of having the interacting voices of Scripture, tradition and culture rather than a monologue by Scripture alone.

A key issue Grenz leaves unresolved is which criteria can therefore be seen as valid in testing the authoritative status of any particular theological tradition. At the very least, tradition needs to be an interactive player subject to other criteria. Acknowledging the input of both Scripture and culture in reaching a decision is useful, but still leaves wide and vague parameters. Openness to pneumatological mediation may reflect a pious and reverent approach to theology, but its hazy boundaries make it hard to either affirm or refute.

Grenz's third source for theological construction is culture. This is his most controversial selection. To Grenz's suggestion that culture is a source for theology, evangelicals are likely to respond that while culture provides the location within which a particular theological system is developed, to suggest that culture is a *source* for theology goes beyond the mandate of evangelical theology.

Because Grenz writes in a nuanced way, it is dangerous to assume that one can respond to his broad categories without carefully examining the meaning he attaches to them.[33] When he suggests culture as a source for theology, at times he seems simply to be calling for a 'culture-sensitive theology', a plea that is neither original nor divisive.[34] At other times he views culture as a 'resource' for theology, another essentially uncontested insight. More often, however, the suggestion is that culture is one of three conversation partners sourcing theology. This latter stance has been the cause of debate among those who have responded to Grenz's work. Bloesch is representative when he writes, 'My problem with Grenz is that he sees mainly promise in cultural achievements and not also deception and self-aggrandizement . . . In a viable biblical, evangelical theology culture is neither deified nor demonized but relativized.'[35]

Grenz's argument is that the Spirit- and community-mediated interaction between culture and Scripture enriches the understanding of Scripture and unearths aspects of biblical truth that would otherwise be overlooked. It also allows the theologian to speak to areas not directly addressed in Scripture. The whole is therefore greater as a result of the interaction, and culture has thus genuinely sourced theological conclusions.[36]

In addition to utilizing Scripture, tradition and culture as sources for theology, Grenz argues that a theology suited to the postmodern situation will utilize three focal motifs, namely the Trinity as a structural motif, community as an integrative motif and eschatology as an orienting motif.[37] He reasons that while the use of Scripture, tradition and culture provide a rounded trio of conversation partners, these should be supplemented by the focal motifs of Trinity, community and eschatology. Placing contemporary theological construction in eschatological perspective, and in this way working backwards from the ultimate *telos* of human existence, helps to address the concerns of the present without being held hostage to them. It ensures that theology retains a prophetically anticipatory character. If the eschaton will see the creation of a community that reflects and interacts with the communion experienced by the triune God, focusing theological construction around Trinity, community and eschatology provides a seamless trio of motifs.

In moving from a single source for theological construction to a trio of sources filtered through three focal motifs, a fundamental methodological problem appears. Grenz uses the image of the three sources acting as conversation partners, but how does one decide if a conversation partner is speaking too loudly? Put differently, if we, for example, say tradition is a source for theological construction, we must ask 'Which tradition?' Some theologians have been willing to make their commitments in this regard clear. Thomas Oden, for example, has proposed that theology draw from a pyramid of sources, with Scripture occupying the wide base of the pyramid and modern theologians the narrow apex.[38] After Scripture come the patristic interpreters of Scripture. Modern sources are given less prominence because, as recent participants in the historical conversation, they have had little time to influence the overall consensus. To the question 'Which tradition should have the dominant voice?' Oden answers that the ancient sources should be given greater weight than recent ones.

While Oden's model does not need to be embraced,[39] he has alerted us to the need for criteria to discern the appropriate 'volume' of each conversation partner. Grenz has made no commitments in this regard, but seems to believe that the natural back and forth of the conversation will help set an appropriate volume for each source. By insisting that Scripture remain the norming norm, the implication is that Scripture has sufficient prominence to mute other sources if they are moving in a direction contrary to Scripture. If this is the case, Grenz is not methodologically transparent in his proposal that there are three conversation partners. A more nuanced approach would acknowledge that while three sources are conversing, they have significantly different amounts of influence.

It is Grenz's use of the term 'source' that is problematic. Claiming that theological construction flows from three sources implies that any of the sources can add to or direct the path taken by the theology constructed. However, a careful reading of Grenz reveals that while he treats Scripture as a genuine source for theology, both tradition and culture serve more as what Macquarrie describes as 'formative factors'.[40] By opting to use the term 'source' Grenz has claimed more for tradition and culture than he is willing to give.[41] Those who have reacted against Grenz have usually accepted Grenz's use of the term 'source' at face value, without observing the significant limitations he places upon both tradition and culture in theological construction. The criticism is therefore often unfounded, but flows from Grenz's misleading terminology.

If it is valid to assert that in Grenz's method Scripture serves as the source for theology and tradition and culture as formative factors, the question arises as to whether Grenz's method represents a genuinely postfoundationalist contribution to theological construction, or if it is better described as a model utilizing a 'chastened' foundationalism in which other voices are encouraged to participate, so long as they essentially harmonize with the lead singer, Scripture.

My conviction is that Grenz has not given sufficient attention to the manner in which the conversation between Scripture, tradition and culture should be undertaken. A more nuanced approach would provide guidelines on the appropriate 'volume' for each conversation partner. Volume might well be related to the topic under investigation.

If Grenz's method is to move beyond the soft (or chastened) foundationalism he embraces, clarification of the rules for the conversation between the sources of theology is needed.

The Case for a Core Conviction

Nicholas Wolterstorff's concept of 'control beliefs' is useful at this point.[42] Wolterstorff notes that certain beliefs, be they religious, philosophical, biblical or other, exercise 'control' over what can and will be believed. He writes, 'Everyone who weighs a theory has certain beliefs as to what constitutes an acceptable *sort* of theory on the matter under consideration. We all have these *control* beliefs.'[43] Control beliefs lead us to reject certain sorts of theories, while they are also instrumental in the theories we devise. He notes, 'We want theories that are consistent with our control beliefs.'[44] Rather than attempt to eliminate control beliefs, Wolterstorff argues that they should be acknowledged and embraced. Thus he suggests that in theology 'the belief-content of the theologian's authentic commitment ought all the while to be functioning also as control over his theory-devising and theory-weighing'.[45] Using Wolterstorff, we can ask what control belief should be adopted to help adjudicate between the differing sources available for theological construction. Examination of Grenz reveals that his control belief is that all theories need to be evaluated in the light of Scripture. To move this beyond foundationalism, he suggests that it is Scripture in interactive conversation with tradition and culture, but this soon leads to a circular argument.[46]

More helpful would be the adoption of a control belief that is allowed to act as a lens through which the contribution of all sources of theological construction is filtered. Attempting to adopt Scripture as both a control belief and a source does not work, as a control belief cannot operate on the same level as a source unless only a single source is allowed. Grenz's attempt to adopt Scripture as one of three sources while at the same time assigning it the role of the control belief[47] is consequently flawed.

The logical question therefore becomes, 'Is there a control belief that can be adopted that is consistent with evangelicalism, which can effectively adjudicate between the differing sources for theological construction?' My proposal is that evangelicalism taps into that which it believes most deeply, namely that the gospel, the *evangel*, is, as the word literally means, good news. This can be expressed in different ways. Some slogans come to mind: 'It isn't the gospel if it isn't good news.' Or Grenz's own contribution: 'participating in what frees'.[48] A suitable synthesis is *the gospel liberates*.

An objection needs to be considered at this point. Is the adoption of a control belief another name for foundationalism? While the question cannot be lightly dismissed, in this instance, it is not. A highly specific and restrictive control belief could be seen as an alternative name for an indisputable foundation, but the control belief adopted is that *the gospel liberates*. While this could be interpreted as a propositional statement (the truth of which needs to be defended), it is better to view it as a statement encapsulating an ethos and projecting a vision. The filtering is on the basis of this expansive ideal. Its edges are soft and allow for the incorporation of new insights. Rather than a foundation from which all other insights flow, the control belief *the gospel liberates* is enriched by its interaction with sources for theological construction such as Scripture, tradition and culture.

The adoption of *the gospel liberates* as the control belief needs further explanation. At the finest moments in their history, evangelicals have been at the forefront of meaningful social change. Evangelicals attribute the abolition of slavery to the evangelical convictions of William Wilberforce and the evangelical Clapham sect. Likewise they attribute measures to protect children, the promotion of religious liberty, and the establishment of multiple humanitarian and educational programmes to those who were motivated by a vision of Christian faith forged within the evangelical camp.[49] An undergirding belief was that *the gospel liberates* those who respond to it, and that this liberation finds expression both in the present moment and throughout eternity.

There is also a shadow side. Certain evangelical groups have been supportive of a right-wing agenda. There have been distressing lapses into racism, sexism, homophobia, militarism, nationalism, ecological and economic exploitation, cultural insensitivity . . . sadly, I could go on.[50]

Evangelicalism's inconsistent track record in the social arena is reflective of an under-developed theological method. While evangelicals usually cite biblical references to justify doctrinal and ethical stances, the lens that drives the selection of the supporting biblical material is rarely acknowledged or examined. Acknowledging and privileging the control belief *the gospel liberates* as the lens through which all assertions are filtered would result in a transparent and consistent method. A critiquing lens calls for accountability for the morality that inevitably flows from all theological construction. While the control belief ultimately critiques what is proposed, the lens adopted shapes construction at all stages.

How would adopting the control belief *the gospel liberates* work in practice?

Each of Grenz's sources for theology is susceptible to the 'which' question. Which reading of Scripture will be privileged? Which tradition will be heeded? Which cultural voices will be heard? Acknowledging a bias[51] towards liberation helps answer these valid questions and allows for a methodological transparency that is otherwise missing.

It also helps to answer the question of the 'volume' of each conversation partner. Privileging a hermeneutic of liberation allows shifting volumes for each conversation partner depending on the issue at stake. We are quick to respond (not uncritically) to those voices that point in a liberating direction. Thus, for example, in ethical reflection on women in leadership, the voice of culture, and especially those cultural voices that are seriously engaged in helping to understand gender and gender discrimination, should be allowed a stronger voice. This is not to attempt to mute the voice of Scripture, but it is to be ready to acknowledge that the discussion of gender in Scripture takes place in a world shaped by patriarchy. A different context sees a different emphasis emerge. Alerted to an outcry from the voice of culture, the conversation deepens as broader biblical themes interact with the insights of the social sciences. The conclusions should not be anticipated in advance, nor should they be fossilized. New insights might lead to the conversation reaching a yet deeper level. Authentic conversation thus takes place within a framework that is genuinely postfoundationalist.

Perhaps, then, with this modification, the potential inherent in Grenz's proposals can be unleashed. Adopting the control belief that *the gospel liberates* could see evangelical theology enter an era of renewal and relevance. And it would certainly stop the silliness of my Calvary Baptist days, where wine-making miracles were morphed into cosy tea parties, and Romans 13 buttressed the status quo, while Amos and the quest for justice were forgotten.

If we are to move beyond toxic faith, we need a robust method that can quickly challenge oppressive conclusions justified by too shallow an appeal to Scripture. Armed with the conviction that *the gospel liberates*, we will enter into discussions on the major ethical challenges of the day with a determination to listen for the voice of the Spirit. We will be quietly confident that as together with other Christians we seek the guidance that comes from Scripture, our traditions and the cultural voice that the Spirit constantly seeks to reform, we will be pointed in a direction that helps us to repeatedly affirm the liberating insight: God is love, God is love, God is love . . .

In Conversation with Becky Oates

In 2014, Becky Oates, together with her husband, Paul, and their four children, moved to India to work with a not-for-profit group dedicated to releasing women from sexual slavery by providing skills that would enable them to embrace viable alternative forms of employment. After a few months, the Oates family realized that they would have to return to Australia. At present their plans to move to India, while not abandoned, are on hold. It has been a costly time for them – both emotionally and financially – and it has raised many questions about guidance. Here are some of Becky's reflections on this time.

Becky, you are writing the answers to my questions in Australia, not India. Why are you here and not there? What happened?

Having spectacularly failed to move my family to India to serve the poor, I am, as you say, writing this sitting at my mother-in-law's kitchen table, given that we sold all our possessions and moved out of our home last year. Having come to the conviction that serving in India was what God was asking of us, we stepped out in faith after a three-year journey of trying to disentangle ourselves from our life in Australia. I have a business here, and having attempted many scenarios that would free me from that responsibility we decided that we would step out in faith and go to India, regardless of our circumstances, and that God would (since he called us) sort it out!

We stepped out of our boat and onto the water with the faith that through him all things are possible and that he would catch us.

I must admit I had imagined that as I stepped out of my boat God would catch me on his high-powered jet ski and whisk me off to a glorious life of serving and living on the edge with God *high five God*.

But in actual fact he caught me in his dinghy and rowed me straight back to the shore that I came from.

What are your dominant emotions when you think about both going to India and returning so soon after leaving?

At the core of who God created me to be, that deep place that only God knows, my heart is screaming and writhing with disappointment that I am not in India. I see Jesus in the poor, and it was the biggest privilege of my life to serve them and live in community with them.

When we realized that in fact God hadn't caught us on his jet ski but that we were going to have to thumb a ride back to Australia, we were physically ill for a week, and have been restless and discontented ever since. How could God so clearly call us to something and then not 'enable it'?

So where do you think God is in the midst of this?

I lost many things during my time in India, but the most remarkable and perhaps most valuable thing I lost was my sense of entitlement. I grew up with the understanding that I was entitled to a certain life. I am entitled to a happy life, a healthy life, a marriage, children; I deserve to feel safe, to have a nourished body, a long successful and rewarding career . . . the list was endless. With that sense of entitlement came disappointment with God when life threw me a curve ball. When God didn't deliver what I was 'entitled to', God became disappointing to me.

It seemed to have escaped my attention that I cannot take a breath without God's gift of life and that I have no control whatsoever.

I now understand that God actually doesn't owe me an explanation.

I understand that life is a struggle, but that God is good.

Any observations on God's guidance?

It has occurred to me that I had lived most of my life with a fairly limited approach to understanding God's guidance.

I had adhered to the 'doors opening/doors closing' type approach. If God opened that door, it must be his will; and if the door was closed, well, he clearly isn't leading me there, and I am absolved of any further responsibility.

It was rubbish, really.

Our journey to India has been confirmed through Scripture, through messages, through our Christian friends, through songs, through words of prophecy and a multitude of other hits in the head with a plank of wood from God. And yet the door will not open. We have pushed and shoved, tried to squeeze under it, tried the fire escape, and yet it won't budge.

As an observer you could understandably question whether God was in fact guiding us to serve in India; perhaps we had it wrong.

Or perhaps God is asking us to step back into his dodgy dinghy and sail back to the poor he so deeply loves, because I don't need a jet ski, and neither does he, because he created the water.

Life is messy, but God is good.

You have lived in close proximity to extreme and desperate poverty. How has that changed you, and what does it make you want to say to our readers?

It's a bit like having new glasses. I see the world through a different filter.

Being poor isn't just about not having enough food or shelter, although that is part of it. It is about not having hope, dignity or freedom. As I write this in air-conditioned comfort, there is a woman in India who is selling her daughter into a lifetime of abuse, because she is so desperately poor she has no choice.

As an entitled foreigner I can look at that and think, 'I would never do that.' It is unthinkable.

It is unthinkable to us because we have no concept of a life without hope, without the freedom of choice.

It is my conviction that God wants to bring freedom. Freedom to those trapped in poverty, and freedom to those trapped in numbing, devious, all-consuming wealth.

If we say we follow Jesus, but live in excessive comfort while our brothers and sisters are suffering unimaginable poverty, are we missing something? Is that how Jesus lived?

My Sunday school teacher taught me a song when I was five:

JOY.

Jesus first, yourself last, and others in between.

I think she nailed it.

To Ponder and Discuss

1. Identify some areas where your beliefs clearly impact your behaviour. Have you ever held flawed beliefs that have led to unhealthy actions? If so, identify some of them.

2. Think about the three conversation partners that Grenz suggests shape what we believe, namely Scripture, tradition and culture. Think about something that you believe strongly. How has it been impacted by each of these voices?

3. Have you ever felt that your faith has seen you defend something that you now consider to be indefensible – perhaps even deeply unjust? If so, what was the problem?

4. What do you think it means to operate from the core conviction that *the gospel liberates*?

11

A Closing Portrait: The Jesus Question

The Jesus Question

As this book draws to a close we come back to its opening question. Are people of faith – and more particularly, those who follow Jesus the Christ – more likely to be like Jekyll or like Hyde? We have seen that faith can pull us in either direction. While our instinct might be to quickly claim that trust in God is always a life-serving force for good, we have been reminded that this is not always the case – indeed, that we cannot even assume that it is the default drive, only overridden in unusual circumstances.

For Christians the question is likely to come back to Jesus. Regardless of what a general belief in God might lead to, they would argue that they are shaped by the fact that they follow Jesus, and therefore an assessment of Jesus and the likely impact of following him is the standard against which the Christian faith must be evaluated. I would therefore like to finish this book by looking at what I call 'the Jesus question'.

The impact of Jesus on human history is rarely disputed. Each time we write the date and note the year we have to ask 'So how many years since what?' Even though it seems unlikely that we have got the answer precisely right, the year is supposed to reflect the number of years since the birth of Jesus. For someone whose public ministry was limited to three years, this is more than just astonishing.

So who is this person around whom human history is dated, and what should the impact of following him be?

I thought it would be helpful to reflect upon some of the descriptors that Jesus selected for himself, and so will briefly comment on the seven memorable 'I am' statements of Jesus: I am the bread of life, I am the light of the world, I am the gate, I am the good shepherd, I am the resurrection and the life, I am the way and the truth and the life, I am the true vine.

The 'I Am' Claims

Two Greek words are used to introduce each of the 'I am' claims of Jesus. Transliterated they are *ego eimi*. They almost certainly relate back to God's self-introduction to Moses in Exodus 3:14, where God chooses to use the name 'I AM' and Moses is told to inform the Israelites, 'I AM has sent me to you.' Greek translations of the Hebrew Bible[1] use the same two Greek words *ego eimi* for 'I am' in Exodus 3:14. In applying the words *ego eimi* to himself, Jesus is implicitly claiming to be divine – to be God. This is a startling assertion, and it led to some strong reactions against Jesus.[2]

As we contemplate each of the 'I am' claims, we get a clearer sense of Jesus' self-understanding. This is the role he sees for himself in the world and in the lives of those who follow him. We will reflect on each of the sayings in turn.

1. *I am the bread of life (John 6:35).* This claim is made shortly after the miraculous feeding of the five thousand. Impressed by Jesus' ability to provide ample calories for the large crowd, people are keen to follow him. Jesus instructs them to see another layer of significance in the miracle, and urges them to 'not work for food that spoils, but for food that endures to eternal life, which the Son of Man will give you. For on him God the Father has placed his seal of approval' (John 6:27). Shortly after saying this he makes his first *ego eimi* claim, 'I am the bread of life. Whoever comes to me will never go hungry, and whoever believes in me will never be thirsty' (John 6:35). The broader context quickly makes it clear

that Jesus is not talking about the provision of food for the body, but primarily spiritual food that nurtures us at a deeper level. To an audience that would have happily settled for a few meals a day, this was stretching. Jesus points to a yearning within the human heart for more, and claims that it can be found in him. The stakes are high, for those who feed on the alternative bread that Jesus speaks of 'will live for ever' (John 6:58).

2. *I am the light of the world (John 8:12)*. This is the second 'I am' declaration. 'When Jesus spoke again to the people, he said, "I am the light of the world. Whoever follows me will never walk in darkness, but will have the light of life."' It led to an immediate outcry from the Pharisees, who dismissed the claim as the delusion of someone reduced to self-testimony. Yet it has never been that easy to dismiss Jesus. The image continues to speak today. The promise of light not just for individuals but for the world is bold. It is a claim that the way of Jesus provides light not just for a few, but for all. Reality cannot be rightly seen or interpreted outside the light that Jesus provides.

3. *I am the gate (or door) (John 10:9)*. The verse following this 'I am' assertion should also be read: 'I am the gate; whoever enters through me will be saved. They will come in and go out, and find pasture. The thief comes only to steal and kill and destroy; I have come that they may have life, and have it to the full.' The implication is that there is one door (or gate) through which to enter to be saved from the surrounding threats which would otherwise destroy. Those who enter it are not disappointed and discover not only pasture to feed and nurture them, but also life in its fullest form. Rather than faith stunting life, this suggests that faith in Jesus not only rescues followers from menacing dangers, but also opens up for them life's richest possibilities.

4. *I am the good shepherd (John 10:11)*. Immediately after making the claim to be the gate that leads to abundant life, Jesus describes himself as the good shepherd. The good shepherd is committed to the welfare of his sheep, even to the point of being willing to die for them. This poignant conversation takes place not long before

the crucifixion and in it Jesus points to the depth of his loyalty to his followers. While not all shepherds protect their flock and act in its best interest, the good shepherd does. Jesus claims the title of the good shepherd for himself, making explicit his willingness to serve those who follow him.

5. *I am the resurrection and the life (John 11:25).* This remarkable 'I am' statement is made when Jesus is confronted by the death of his friend Lazarus. Shortly before he raises Lazarus from the dead, Jesus says, 'I am the resurrection and the life. The one who believes in me will live, even though they die; and whoever lives by believing in me will never die.' If death is life's greatest foe, the allegation must be investigated. It promises life beyond the grave.

6. *I am the way and the truth and the life (John 14:6).* Perhaps this is the most exclusive of Jesus' claims. He states, 'I am the way and the truth and the life. No one comes to the Father except through me.' The trio of titles should be noted – the way, the truth and the life. Add these together and you realize that Jesus does not view following him as a pleasant additional bonus to life – something you can take or leave. All of reality is tied up in him. Following him is about a path for life, ultimate truth and life at its fullest.

7. *I am the true vine (John 15:1).* To those afraid that commitment to Jesus will lead to a fruitless, wasted life, Jesus promises that he is the true vine, and that when we remain connected to him, our lives will be productive. A process of pruning might be required, but it is never arbitrary, but focused on achieving that which matters most.

Some will read the 'I am' list and conclude that the case is proved. Jesus was delusional and succumbed to serious bouts of self-aggrandizement. Of course, if Jesus isn't actually the Son of God, this conclusion is justified. We could state it even more strongly. If Jesus is not who he claims to be, he is a religious fraud – indeed, the greatest religious fraud in history. A nice person doesn't declare themselves to be the way, the truth and the life, nor do they suggest that they are the light of the world.

Assessing the worthiness of Jesus has to relate back to the question of truth. Is he who he says he is, the Son of God?

Those who conclude that he is not have little choice but to declare Christianity toxic. Based upon a myth, Christianity is, they will surely declare, a hoax of astonishing proportions. Human history has been shaped by a lie, and the sooner it is rectified the sooner we can face reality and respond to it appropriately. It would be outrageous to insist that we take seriously the ethical teaching of someone who was so deeply flawed and so out of touch with reality.

True, some would try to soften this conclusion and argue that you should sift the good from the bad. Jesus might have been mistaken as to his identity, but much of his teaching was insightful. If we edit out some of his more extreme statements and claims, we arrive at a wholesome vision of life. While this view has its advocates, I do not find it very convincing. Throughout history, religious tricksters have always had sufficient credibility in some areas to deceive the gullible. If this is what we are claiming for Jesus, it is not very impressive.

Perhaps it was not Jesus who claimed to be divine, but his later followers who tried to portray him in this light. Jesus then might have been a controversial but brilliant itinerant preacher and teacher who was executed for advocating an alternative way of living. After his death, those impacted by his teaching slowly raised the bar, so that in the end his status soared, finally settling on the setting of God. If this is the case, it was not Jesus who was confused as to his status, but his followers, many of whom were prepared to die for the myth they created. Naturally, they not only had to insert his claims to divinity, but they also had to fabricate the accounts of the miracles, including the greatest miracle of all, the resurrection. While not absolutely impossible, the likelihood of this is slight. If this myth creation had led to a life of ease and comfort for Jesus' disciples, it could be entertained as an option. However, it had the exact opposite effect, leading to their persecution, ostracism and death. It is hard to understand why they would so doggedly hold on to a myth they knew they had created.

This brings us back to the first option – that the 'I am' statements are true, and that Jesus is indeed who he said he was.

If you conclude that Jesus is the Son of God, the implications that flow from the 'I am' statements are staggering and must be taken with the utmost seriousness. They suggest a pathway to a transforming vision of life; a life filled with the promise of light, truth and direction . . . a vision of fruitful living, and the settled confidence of victory over death. Such a confidence provides the motivation and courage to live a life a little less ordinary. Rather than retreating into escapism, we can embrace the gift of life confident that the good shepherd has come that we might have life, and life in all its fullness. There is nothing toxic about this.

To be sure, nothing would be more disappointing than if those who follow the one they believe to be the bread of life allow themselves to adopt poisonous versions of faith. Genuine followers of Jesus must willingly and courageously follow the good shepherd, for the good shepherd provides bread and life and light, not only for them, but for the whole world.

In Conversation with Peter Christofides

Dr Peter Christofides lectures in New Testament at Vose Seminary. He has also been involved in a suicide prevention programme.

Peter, which of the 'I am' statements strikes you most forcefully, and why?

When I think of the associations of all the 'I am' statements that Jesus made, I am most forcefully impressed by 'I am the bread of life' (John 6:35). When I ponder the basic simple element of bread, I am amazed by how important it is for life! Because of the major need for it and Jesus claiming to be it, it is a compelling and captivating reality to meditate upon. When I consider that it is bread that is the most staple of foods, I realize that he is the one who fulfils, and sustains, my basic longing in life.

Simple bread can fill and sustain us for hours. Also, it is not when it is on the shelf or in the freezer that it is most effective, but when it is consumed by me. This 'consumption of Jesus' is most applicable 'in me'. Walking past the bakery and inhaling that great aroma does not quench my hunger. It is also not in the chewing of the bread that I am fully satisfied; it is in the swallowing and digesting that I am gratified. It is in the 'fresh bread' that I find the greatest satisfaction and gain the most strength.

As a New Testament scholar, do you think we can trust the Gospels to be an accurate account of the life, ministry and teaching of Jesus, and why?

If I think of what the word 'gospel' means, I am taken to the Greek word *euangelion*, which means 'good news'. As Christians we believe that the four recorded Gospels, namely, Matthew, Mark, Luke and John, are a record of the life of Jesus. Many questions are often raised regarding the reliability of the Gospels in the Bible. Why were these four Gospels not exactly the same? Who were these authors? How can we be sure that they were in a position to know what really happened in the life of Jesus? Volumes could be written addressing each of these questions. However, we will discover that, despite years of attacks on their credibility, it is still reasonable to believe that the authors of the four Gospels had access to reliable biographical information about Jesus and that that information has been faithfully transmitted to us over the centuries. Apart from the rigorous process that the four Gospels needed to go through before they were accepted as trustworthy, we see that each of these writers who accurately wrote about the life, ministry and teaching of Jesus was, first, a prophet of God. Second, these writers were authenticated by miracles to confirm their message. Third, they spoke the truth about the life of Christ, with no falsehood or contradiction. Fourth, each of these four Gospels demonstrates a divine capacity to transform lives. And fifth, each of these four Gospels was accepted as God's Word by the people to whom it was first delivered. Indeed, these Gospels can be trusted as they have survived the test of time.

Your faith in Jesus has led you to be involved in some practical programmes of care. Tell us about your involvement in the suicide prevention programme.

I am of Greek origin, and one of the reasons I moved from Johannesburg to Darwin was because of the large Greek population in Darwin (about sixteen thousand people). Most of these Greeks are involved in the construction industry. In trying to reach out to them, I discovered anxiety, depression and much mental unwellness. It sometimes led to suicide. I was involved in an early intervention suicide prevention and capacity building programme. It was founded on the vision to enhance resilience for apprentices, trainees and workers in industry, while at the same time strengthening the support role of their employers. The whole philosophy behind what I was doing and getting involved with is the reality that wellness, building resilience and life skills through mental health promotion involves a holistic viewpoint that helps people cope with life's challenges.

Having spent many years as a chaplain, I witnessed far too often the devastating impact of suicide. It not only affects family and friends, but also co-workers and whole workplaces are touched. Through the programme I was able to provide some practical tools and tips to deal with what for too long has been an uncomfortable and highly stigmatized area of health. I helped people recognize vulnerability, mental ill-health, the signs and symptoms, and what is helpful and not helpful, so that people would not have any regrets as to whether they could have made a difference. It was challenging!

Why do you think people sometimes get so desperate that they contemplate ending it all?

We live in a world where people find it difficult to juggle their lives. We face global economic uncertainty. Mental health problems are an increasing concern and are currently growing. Mental health is a state of well-being. The way we see ourselves and the world around us affects our emotional, psychological, physical and spiritual well-being. We all experience bad days when our motivation may not be at its peak; we may feel stress due to deadlines, work obligations or family pressures. When these realities of life squeeze us, they cause stresses and affect our mental health. We do not always recognize the amount of stress that ordinary life events can have on us – such as moving house, marriage or even retirement. But when this stress goes beyond a certain point, our capacity to cope reduces. This sense of anxiety impacts our ability to concentrate and focus on what we are doing. Feeling consistently stressed and anxious over a period of time limits our ability to perform and also may result in negative physical and emotional outcomes. Sadly, these stressors do not usually occur in isolation but build up. In today's hectic life, time for recovery between stressful situations can be harder to find. Finding something that can take your mind to another space for a short time while you relax and recharge your batteries is often hard to find – hence the desperation that leads to the contemplation to end it all.

What do you think are some signs that people have adopted a genuine life-serving faith in Jesus?

In the natural world, fruit is the result of a healthy plant producing what it was designed to produce. In the Bible, the word 'fruit' is often used to describe a person's outward actions that result from the condition of the heart. Good fruit is that which is produced by the Holy Spirit. Galatians 5:22–3 gives us a starting place: the fruit (the word is singular – hence, all Christians are to have all the fruit, unlike the gifts of the Holy Spirit) of his Spirit is love, joy, peace, patience, kindness, goodness, faithfulness, gentleness and self-control. The more we allow the Holy Spirit free rein in our lives, the more this fruit is evident – and results in our serving one another.

As disciples of Christ, we must stay firmly connected to him to remain spiritually productive. We need daily surrender, daily communication, and daily repentance and connection with the Holy Spirit in order to 'live by the Spirit, and . . . not gratify the desires of the flesh' (Gal. 5:16). Staying intimately connected to the True

Vine is the only way to 'bear fruit in old age' (Ps. 92:14), to 'run and not grow weary' (Isa. 40:31) and to 'not become weary in doing good' (Gal. 6:9).

Without being overly simplistic, to stay firmly connected, we need to develop a life of prayer. This is of great benefit as it deepens conversation with God and allows us to draw from the one who discerns our life and directs it in order to produce the signs of a genuine life-serving faith in Jesus.

To Ponder and Discuss

1. What do you make of the claims of Jesus? Do you find them credible, or do you think they are deliberately deceiving, deluded or perhaps doctored by his early followers? Are there some other options?
2. If Jesus isn't the Son of God, can anything still be salvaged for Christianity, or should it be rejected as an unhelpful and restrictive myth?
3. If Jesus is the Son of God, what implications should this have for our daily living?
4. What impact does faith have on your life? Has it led you to 'life in all its fullness'? If not, do you think it could?

Bibliography

Allport, G.W. *The Individual and His Religion: A Psychological Interpretation* (New York: Macmillan, 1950).

———. 'Religion and Prejudice.' *The Crane Review* 2 (1959): pp. 1–10.

———, and M.J. Ross. 'Personal Religious Orientation and Prejudice.' *Journal of Personality and Social Psychology* 5 (1967): pp. 432–43.

Andrews, Dave. *People of Compassion* (Blackburn, VIC: TEAR Australia, 2008).

Batson, C. Daniel, Patricia Schoenrade and W. Larry Ventis. *Religion and the Individual: A Social-Psychological Perspective* (New York: Oxford University Press, rev. edn, 1993).

Bebbington, David. *Evangelicalism in Modern Britain: A History from the 1730s to the 1980s* (Grand Rapids: Baker, 1989).

Bellah, Robert N., Richard Madsen, William M. Sullivan, Ann Swidler and Steven M. Tipton. *Habits of the Heart: Individualism and Commitment in American Life* (Berkeley: University of California Press, 1985).

Berger, Peter L. *Pyramids of Sacrifice: Political Ethics and Social Change* (New York: Anchor, 1976).

Bindley, T.H. *The Apology of Tertullian for the Christians* (Oxford: Parker, 1890).

Blanchard, John. *Does God Believe in Atheists?* (Darlington: Evangelical Press, 2000).

Bloesch, Donald G. 'Donald Bloesch Responds: On Grenz.' Pages 184–7 in *Evangelical Theology in Transition: Theologians in Dialogue with Donald Bloesch* (ed. Elmer M. Colyer; Downers Grove: IVP, 1999).

Boisen, Anton T. *The Exploration of the Inner World: A Study of Mental Disorder and Religious Experience* (New York: Harper Torchbooks, 1936).

Bonhoeffer, Dietrich. *Ethics* (trans. Neville Horton Smith; New York: Macmillan, 1965).

————. *Life Together: Prayerbook of the Bible*, Vol. 5, *Dietrich Bonhoeffer Works* (trans. Daniel W. Bloesch and James H. Burtness; Minneapolis: Fortress, 2005).

Boulton, Matthew Myer. 'Unholy Rites: What's Wrong with Worship?' *Christian Century* 126, no. 2 (2009): pp. 30–33.

Brand, Chad O. 'Defining Evangelicalism.' Pages 281–304 in *Reclaiming the Center: Confronting Evangelical Accommodation in Postmodern Times* (ed. Millard J. Erickson, Paul Kjoss Helseth and Justin Taylor; Wheaton: Crossway, 2004).

Campbell, Ted A. 'The "Wesleyan Quadrilateral": The Story of a Modern Methodist Myth.' *Methodist History* 29 (1991): pp. 87–95.

Carson, D.A. *The Gagging of God: Christianity Confronts Pluralism* (Grand Rapids: Zondervan, 1996).

————. *For the Love of God*, Vol. 1 (Nottingham: IVP, 1998).

————. 'Domesticating the Gospel: A Review of Grenz's Renewing the Center.' Pages 33–55 in *Reclaiming the Center: Confronting Evangelical Accommodation in Postmodern Times* (ed. Millard J. Erickson, Paul Kjoss Helseth and Justin Taylor; Wheaton: Crossway, 2004).

Chesterton, G.K. *What's Wrong with the World* (London: Cassell, 1910).

Cohen, David. *Why O Lord? Praying Our Sorrows* (Milton Keynes: Paternoster, 2013).

de Gruchy, John W., and Charles Villa-Vicencio, eds. *Apartheid Is a Heresy* (Grand Rapids: Eerdmans, 1983).

Erickson, Millard J. *The Evangelical Left: Encountering Postconservative Evangelical Theology* (Grand Rapids: Baker, 1997).

———. 'On Flying in Theological Fog.' Pages 323–47 in *Reclaiming the Center: Confronting Evangelical Accommodation in Postmodern Times* (ed. Millard J. Erickson, Paul Kjoss Helseth and Justin Taylor; Wheaton: Crossway, 2004).

Freud, Sigmund. *The Future of an Illusion* (Seattle: Pacific, 2010).

Goffee, Rob, and Gareth Jones. 'Creating the Best Workplace on Earth.' *Harvard Business Review* (May 2013) https://hbr.org/2013/05/creating-the-best-workplace-on-earth.

Green, Michael. *Evangelism in the Early Church* (London: Hodder & Stoughton, 1970).

Greene, Mark. *Fruitfulness on the Frontline: Making a Difference Where You Are* (Nottingham: IVP, 2014).

Greenleaf, Robert K. *Servant Leadership: A Journey into the Nature of Legitimate Power and Greatness* (New York: Paulist Press, 1977).

Grenz, Stanley J. *Revisioning Evangelical Theology: A Fresh Agenda for the Twenty First Century* (Downers Grove: Inter-Varsity Press, 1993).

———. *Theology for the Community of God* (Nashville: Broadman & Holman, 1994).

———. 'Culture and Spirit: The Role of Cultural Context in Theological Reflection.' *Asbury Theological Journal* 55, no. 2 (2000): pp. 37–51.

———. 'What Does Hollywood Have to Do with Wheaton? The Place of (Pop) Culture in Theological Reflection.' *Journal of the Evangelical Theological Society* 43, no. 2 (2000): pp. 303–14.

———. 'Participating in What Frees: The Concept of Truth in the Postmodern Context.' *Review and Expositor* 100 (Fall 2003): pp. 687–93.

———, and John R. Franke. *Beyond Foundationalism: Shaping Theology in a Postmodern Context* (Louisville: Westminster John Knox Press, 2001).

Gushee, David P. *Changing Our Mind* (Canton: Read the Spirit, 2014).

Harmon, Steven R. 'The Authority of the Community (of All the Saints): Toward a Postmodern Baptist Hermeneutic of Tradition.' *Review and Expositor* 100 (2003): pp. 587–621.

Harris, Brian. 'Beyond Bebbington: The Quest for an Evangelical Identity in a Postmodern Era.' *Churchman* 122, no. 3 (2008): pp. 201–19.

———. 'Why Method Matters: Insights from the Theological Method of Stanley J. Grenz.' *Crucible* 2, no. 1 (2009).

———. *The Tortoise Usually Wins: Biblical Reflections on Quiet Leadership for Reluctant Leaders* (Milton Keynes: Paternoster, 2013).

———. *The Big Picture: Building Blocks of a Christian World View* (Milton Keynes: Paternoster, 2015).

Hart, David Bentley. *Atheist Delusions: The Christian Revolution and Its Fashionable Enemies* (New Haven: Yale University Press, 2009).

Helseth, Paul Kjoss. 'Are Postconservative Evangelicals Fundamentalists? Postconservative Evangelicalism, Old Princeton and the Rise of Neo-Fundamentalism.' Pages 223–50 in *Reclaiming the Center: Confronting Evangelical Accommodation in Postmodern Times* (ed. Millard J. Erickson, Paul Kjoss Helseth and Justin Taylor; Wheaton: Crossway, 2004).

Hills, Peter, Leslie J. Francis, Michael Argyle and Chris J. Jackson. 'Primary Personality Trait Correlates of Religious Practice and Orientation.' *Personality and Individual Differences* 36 (2004): pp. 61–73.

Hitchens, Christopher. *God Is Not Great: How Religion Poisons Everything* (New York: Twelve, 2007).

Jamieson, Alan. *A Churchless Faith: Faith Journeys Beyond Evangelical, Pentecostal and Charismatic Churches* (Wellington: Philip Garside Publishing, 2000).

Jenkins, Philip. *Laying Down the Sword: Why We Can't Ignore the Bible's Violent Verses* (New York: Harper One, 2011).

Kant, Immanuel. *Religion within the Limits of Reason Alone* (trans. Theodore M. Greene and Hoyt H. Hudson; New York: Harper & Row, 1960).

Kinnaman, David, and Gabe Lyons. *Unchristian: What a New Generation Really Thinks about Christianity . . . And Why It Matters* (Grand Rapids: Baker, 2007).

Lennox, John. *God's Undertaker: Has Science Buried God?* (Oxford: Lion, 2009).

Lewis, C.S. *Mere Christianity: A Revised and Amplified Edition* (San Francisco: Harper, 2001).

Macquarrie, John. *Principles of Christian Theology* (London: SCM, rev. edn, 1977).

Marx, Karl. *Critique of Hegel's Philosophy of Right* (Chicago: Aristeus Books, 2012).

Maslach, Christina. *Burnout: The Cost of Caring* (Paramus: Prentice Hall, 1982).

McKnight, Scot. *The Jesus Creed: Loving God, Loving Others* (Brewster: Paraclete Press, 2004).

Neyrinck, Bart, Willy Lens, Maarten Vansteenkiste and Bart Soenens. 'Updating Allport's and Batson's Framework of Religious Orientations: A Reevaluation from the Perspective of Self-Determination Theory and Wulff's Social Cognitive Model.' *Journal for the Scientific Study of Religion* 49, no. 3 (2010): pp. 425–38.

Nicholi, Armand M. *The Question of God: C.S. Lewis and Sigmund Freud Debate God, Love, Sex and the Meaning of Life* (New York: Free Press, 2002).

Nieuwhof, Carey. '9 Signs You're Burning out in Leadership.' (2013) http://careynieuwhof.com/2013/07/9-signs-youre-burning-out-in-leadership/ (accessed June 2015).

Oden, Thomas C. *The Word of Life* (San Francisco: Harper & Row, 1992).

Otto, Rudolf. *The Idea of the Holy* (trans. John W. Harvey; Oxford: Oxford University Press, 2nd edn, 1958).

Placher, William C., ed. *Callings: Twenty Centuries of Christian Wisdom on Vocation* (Grand Rapids: Eerdmans, 2005).

Read, Geoff. *Ministry Burnout* (Cambridge: Grove Books, 2009).

Scazzero, Peter. *Emotionally Healthy Spirituality* (Nashville: Thomas Nelson, 2006).

Schmidt, Alvin J. *Under the Influence: How Christianity Transformed Culture* (Grand Rapids: Zondervan, 2001).

Seibert, Eric A. *Disturbing Divine Behavior* (Minneapolis: Fortress, 2009).

Smith, James K.A. 'The Closing of the Book: Pentecostals, Evangelicals, and the Sacred Writings.' *Journal of Pentecostal Theology* 11 (1997): pp. 49–71.

Stott, John. *Evangelical Truth: A Personal Plea for Unity* (Leicester: Inter-Varsity Press, 1999).

Strom, Mark. *Arts of the Wise Leader* (Sydney: Sophos, 2007).

Thielicke, Helmut. *The Ethics of Sex* (trans. John W. Doberstein; Grand Rapids: Baker, 1964).

Travis, William G. 'Pietism and the History of American Evangelicalism.' Pages 251–79 in *Reclaiming the Center: Confronting Evangelical Accommodation in Postmodern Times* (ed. Millard J. Erickson, Paul Kjoss Helseth and Justin Taylor; Wheaton: Crossway, 2004).

Trible, Phyllis. *Texts of Terror: Literary-Feminist Readings of Biblical Narratives* (Philadelphia: Fortress, 1984).

Turak, August. *The Business Secrets of the Trappist Monks* (New York: Columbia Business School, 2013).

Van Huyssteen, J. Wentzel. 'Tradition and the Task of Theology.' *Theology Today* 55, no. 2 (1998): pp. 213–28.

Wallis, Jim. *The Call to Conversion* (Herts: Lion, 1981).

Wilcox, W. Bradford, and Elizabeth Williamson. 'The Cultural Contradictions of Mainline Family Ideology and Practice.' Pages 37–55 in *American Religions and the Family* (ed. Don S. Browning and David. A. Clairmont; New York: Columbia University Press, 2007).

Wolterstorff, Nicholas. *Reason within the Bounds of Religion* (Grand Rapids: Eerdmans, 1976).

Wright, Bradley R.E. *Christians Are Hate-Filled Hypocrites . . . And Other Lies You've Been Told* (Minneapolis: Bethany, 2010).

Endnotes

1. Jekyll or Hyde: More Than a Minor Dilemma

1 Christopher Hitchens, *God Is Not Great: How Religion Poisons Everything* (New York: Twelve, 2007).

2 G.K. Chesterton, *What's Wrong with the World* (London: Cassell, 1910), Part 1, Ch. 5.

3 David Kinnaman and Gabe Lyons, *Unchristian: What a New Generation Really Thinks about Christianity . . . And Why It Matters* (Grand Rapids: Baker, 2007).

4 D.A. Carson, *For the Love of God*, Vol. 1 (Nottingham: IVP, 1998), 23 January.

5 A simple but thought-provoking introduction to the topic is found in Dave Andrews, *People of Compassion* (Blackburn, VIC: TEAR Australia, 2008).

6 While it can be argued that we should distinguish between the Christ story and the history of the churches founded as a result of that story, in practice this is difficult to do. It is however true that the Christ story could (and probably should) serve as the filter to determine the faithfulness or otherwise of the churches formed following their mandate to serve as Christ's body on earth.

7 So, for example, Jim Wallis, speaking of the mixed legacy of evangelicalism, laments, 'Evangelicals in [the twentieth] century have a history of going along with the culture on the big issues and taking their stand on the smaller issues. That has been one of the serious problems of evangelical religion. Today, many evangelicals no longer just acquiesce to the culture on the larger economic and political issues, but actively promote the culture's worst values on these matters.' Jim Wallis, *The Call to Conversion* (Herts: Lion, 1981), p. 25.

8 John Stott, *Evangelical Truth: A Personal Plea for Unity* (Leicester: Inter-Varsity Press, 1999), pp. 21–4.

2. What about Other Religions?

1 Rudolf Otto, *The Idea of the Holy* (trans. John W. Harvey; Oxford: Oxford University Press, 2nd edn, 1958).

2 This point is a quote from an earlier publication of mine, Brian Harris, *The Big Picture: Building Blocks of a Christian World View* (Milton Keynes: Paternoster, 2015), p. 50.

3 Ibid., pp. 31–46.

4 Ibid., pp. 38–9.

3. Marx: Faith as Escapism

1 Karl Marx, *Critique of Hegel's Philosophy of Right* (Chicago: Aristeus Books, 2012), 4; ibid.

2 For some thoughtful reflections on this, see Matthew Myer Boulton, 'Unholy Rites: What's Wrong with Worship?', *Christian Century* 126, no. 2 (2009).

3 As he would prefer to be unidentified, I have changed his name.

4 Matt. 17:1–21; Mark 9:2–29; Luke 9:28–43.

5 David Cohen has written a useful book on the pastoral use of lament psalms (or psalms of distress) in helping people come to terms with loss and disappointment. David Cohen, *Why O Lord? Praying Our Sorrows* (Milton Keynes: Paternoster, 2013).

6 Or marginal reading: 'valley of the shadow of death'.

7 Bonhoeffer writes, 'Every human idealized image that is brought into the Christian community is a hindrance to genuine community and must be broken up so that genuine community can survive. Those who love their dream of a Christian community more than the Christian community itself become destroyers of that Christian community even though their personal intentions may be ever so honest, earnest, and sacrificial.' Dietrich Bonhoeffer, *Life Together: Prayerbook of the Bible*, Vol. 5, *Dietrich Bonhoeffer Works* (trans. Daniel W. Bloesch and James H. Burtness; Minneapolis: Fortress, 2005), p. 36.

8 Some of this section is a lightly edited version of the first chapter of my book *The Big Picture*.

9 Stanley J. Grenz and John R. Franke, *Beyond Foundationalism: Shaping Theology in a Postmodern Context* (Louisville: Westminster John Knox Press, 2001).

4. Freud: Faith as Illusion

1 Sigmund Freud, *The Future of an Illusion* (Seattle: Pacific 2010), p. 55.

2 Cited in Peter Hills et al., 'Primary Personality Trait Correlates of Religious Practice and Orientation', *Personality and Individual Differences* 36 (2004): p. 62.

3   It is worth noting that Freud distinguished between an illusion and an error. An illusion is not necessarily an error, but is something that arises from our inner wishes. It could, however, be true, regardless of its origin. It is therefore possible that Christianity is a true illusion, in the sense that it meets our deepest inner wishes but also corresponds with reality. Not that this is what Freud suggests, but he does make it clear that saying that religion is an illusion is not the same as saying that religious beliefs are false.

4   Though note my qualification in footnote 3 above, that Freud differentiated between an illusion and an error, concluding that an illusion is not necessarily an error.

5   See, for example, John Blanchard, *Does God Believe in Atheists?* (Darlington: Evangelical Press, 2000); David Bentley Hart, *Atheist Delusions: The Christian Revolution and Its Fashionable Enemies* (New Haven: Yale University Press, 2009); John Lennox, *God's Undertaker: Has Science Buried God?* (Oxford: Lion, 2009); C.S. Lewis, *Mere Christianity: A Revised and Amplified Edition* (San Francisco: Harper, 2001); Armand M. Nicholi, *The Question of God: C.S. Lewis and Sigmund Freud Debate God, Love, Sex and the Meaning of Life* (New York: Free Press, 2002).

6   G.W. Allport, *The Individual and His Religion: A Psychological Interpretation* (New York: Macmillan, 1950); G.W. Allport, 'Religion and Prejudice', *The Crane Review* 2 (1959); G.W. Allport and M.J. Ross, 'Personal Religious Orientation and Prejudice', *Journal of Personality and Social Psychology* 5 (1967).

7   Allport, *The Individual and His Religion*; Allport, 'Religion and Prejudice'; Allport and Ross, 'Personal Religious Orientation and Prejudice'.

8   See C. Daniel Batson, Patricia Schoenrade and W. Larry Ventis, *Religion and the Individual: A Social-Psychological Perspective* (New York: Oxford University Press, rev. edn, 1993), pp. 161–77. Some feel the concepts are in need of re-evaluation. See Bart Neyrinck et al., 'Updating Allport's and Batson's Framework of Religious Orientations: A Reevaluation from the Perspective of Self-Determination Theory and Wulff's Social Cognitive Model', *Journal for the Scientific Study of Religion* 49, no. 3 (2010).

9   See ch. 8, Harris, *The Big Picture*.

5. Hitchens: Faith as Poisonous

1   Kinnaman and Lyons, *Unchristian*.

2   Bradley R.E. Wright, *Christians Are Hate-Filled Hypocrites . . . And Other Lies You've Been Told* (Minneapolis: Bethany, 2010), p. 133. W. Bradford Wilcox and Elizabeth Williamson, 'The Cultural Contradictions of Mainline Family Ideology

and Practice', in *American Religions and the Family* (ed. Don S. Browning and David. A. Clairmont; New York: Columbia University Press, 2007), p. 50.

3   A significant example is David P. Gushee, *Changing Our Mind* (Canton: Read the Spirit, 2014).

4   Anton T. Boisen, *The Exploration of the Inner World: A Study of Mental Disorder and Religious Experience* (New York: Harper Torchbooks, 1936), p. 10.

5   Philip Jenkins, *Laying Down the Sword: Why We Can't Ignore the Bible's Violent Verses* (New York: Harper One, 2011), p. 21.

6   Eric A. Seibert, *Disturbing Divine Behavior* (Minneapolis: Fortress, 2009).

7   Scot McKnight, *The Jesus Creed: Loving God, Loving Others* (Brewster: Paraclete Press, 2004).

6. And What About . . . ? Some Other Temptations

1   I have written on the topic of leadership in far greater detail in my book *The Tortoise Usually Wins* and have lightly edited parts of Chapter 2 from that book for this section. Brian Harris, *The Tortoise Usually Wins: Biblical Reflections on Quiet Leadership for Reluctant Leaders* (Milton Keynes: Paternoster, 2013).

2   I use the term 'models' (plural) intentionally, as the Bible offers many portraits of leadership. They are richly nuanced, and cannot be neatly reduced into one tidy model, though basic themes recur repeatedly (such as servant leadership).

3   Robert K. Greenleaf, *Servant Leadership: A Journey into the Nature of Legitimate Power and Greatness* (New York: Paulist Press, 1977), p. 8.

4   This is a popular rendition from Tertullian's *Apologeticus*, ch. 50, written in 197. T.H. Bindley translates the Latin as 'We spring up in greater numbers as we are mown down by you: the blood of the Christians is a source of new life.' T.H. Bindley, *The Apology of Tertullian for the Christians* (Oxford: Parker, 1890), p. 82.

5   Peter L. Berger, *Pyramids of Sacrifice: Political Ethics and Social Change* (New York: Anchor, 1976).

6   Peter Scazzero, *Emotionally Healthy Spirituality* (Nashville: Thomas Nelson, 2006), pp. 34–5.

7   Geoff Read, *Ministry Burnout* (Cambridge: Grove Books, 2009), p. 11.

8   David Bebbington, *Evangelicalism in Modern Britain: A History from the 1730s to the 1980s* (Grand Rapids: Baker, 1989), pp. 10–12.

9   Christina Maslach, *Burnout: The Cost of Caring* (Paramus: Prentice Hall, 1982).

10   Rob Goffee and Gareth Jones, 'Creating the Best Workplace on Earth', *Harvard Business Review* (May 2013) https://hbr.org/2013/05/creating-the-best-work-place-on-earth.

11 Carey Nieuwhof, '9 Signs You're Burning out in Leadership' (2013) http://careynieuwhof.com/2013/07/9-signs-youre-burning-out-in-leadership/ (accessed June 2015).

7. Contours for a Transforming Christian World View

1 What follows is a lightly edited version of parts of the opening chapter of my book *The Big Picture*. The topics introduced here are developed at chapter length in that book, and, hopefully, this sampler will whet your appetite to read it.

2 Helmut Thielicke, *The Ethics of Sex* (trans. John W. Doberstein; Grand Rapids: Baker, 1964), p. 26.

3 This is essentially the position adopted by Bonhoeffer in the opening chapter of *Ethics*. Dietrich Bonhoeffer, *Ethics* (trans. Neville Horton Smith; New York: Macmillan, 1965).

4 See, for example, Robert Bellah's *Habits of the Heart*. One of the issues high-lighted in *Habits of the Heart* is the link between religion and individualism. The privatization of faith, be it the plea from evangelicals to come into a personal (individual) relationship with God, or the more liberal invitation to worship God in whatever shape or form the individual chooses to conceive the Divine, tends to see the emphasis fall back to individual response rather than to community mediation. While individualism might lead to ownership of decisions taken, it can also lead to a sense of isolation and alienation. Robert N. Bellah et al, *Habits of the Heart: Individualism and Commitment in American Life* (Berkeley: University of California Press, 1985).

5 Conversionism is one of the four distinctives cited by Bebbington as forming a quadrilateral of priorities for evangelicalism. The others are activism, biblicism and crucicentrism. Bebbington, *Evangelicalism in Modern Britain*, pp. 2–3.

6 Alan Jamieson, *A Churchless Faith: Faith Journeys Beyond Evangelical, Pentecostal and Charismatic Churches* (Wellington: Philip Garside Publishing, 2000).

8. Life-Serving Faith: Transformed Individuals

1 The material under this heading is a lightly edited version of the summary I provide in a section of Chapter 4 of my book *The Big Picture*.

2 Orthopathy is sometimes used as a term to describe the treatment of disease without the use of drugs, and is linked to the Natural Hygiene movement, an

alternative medical belief. This is not the sense in which it is being used here.

3   August Turak, *The Business Secrets of the Trappist Monks* (New York: Columbia Business School, 2013), pp. 29–31.

4   See, for example, Matt. 28:18–20 and Acts 1:6–8.

5   A similar sentiment is expressed in 1 Cor. 10:31 and Col. 3:17.

6   William C. Placher, ed., *Callings: Twenty Centuries of Christian Wisdom on Vocation* (Grand Rapids: Eerdmans, 2005), p. 2.

7   For those who want to explore this topic further, an accessible and practical introduction is Mark Greene, *Fruitfulness on the Frontline: Making a Difference Where You Are* (Nottingham: IVP, 2014).

9. Life-Serving Faith: The Global Impact

1   Alvin J. Schmidt, *Under the Influence: How Christianity Transformed Culture* (Grand Rapids: Zondervan, 2001), p. 14.

2   Ibid., p. 12.

3   Michael Green, *Evangelism in the Early Church* (London: Hodder & Stoughton, 1970), p. 13.

4   Ibid.

5   Ibid., p. 19.

6   Bindley, *The Apology of Tertullian for the Christians* (Oxford: Parker, 1890), p. 82.

7   A sober reading of 1 Corinthians quickly squashes any naivety about the life of the early church. Few contemporary churches have as many problems as that troubled community.

8   Mark Strom, *Arts of the Wise Leader* (Sydney: Sophos, 2007), p. 73.

9   Name changed to preserve confidentiality.

10 In the early days of the AIDS epidemic it was assumed that carriers could transmit their disease far more easily than turned out to be the case.

10. Theology Matters: The Case for a Core Conviction

1   Published as Brian Harris, 'Why Method Matters: Insights from the Theological Method of Stanley J. Grenz', *Crucible* 2, no. 1 (2009).

2   David Bebbington classifies these four concerns, which he calls biblicism, cruci-centrism, conversionism and activism, as a quadrilateral of priorities under-girding evangelicalism. Bebbington, *Evangelicalism in Modern Britain*, pp. 2–3.

For an exploration of Bebbington's quadrilateral and its current relevance for evangelicalism, see Brian Harris, 'Beyond Bebbington: The Quest for an Evangelical Identity in a Postmodern Era', *Churchman* 122, no. 3 (2008).

3 Grenz and Franke, *Beyond Foundationalism*, p. 13.

4 I have changed the name lest I inadvertently offend any of the wonderful people who were there at that time.

5 Name changed.

6 Boisen, *Exploration of the Inner World*, p. 10.

7 Such sermons were common in South Africa during the apartheid era.

8 I realize this gives a slightly different slant to the phrase coined by Phyllis Trible, but I think it is appropriate. Phyllis Trible, *Texts of Terror: Literary-Feminist Readings of Biblical Narratives* (Philadelphia: Fortress, 1984).

9 The denunciation of apartheid as a heresy during the 1982 Ottawa meeting of the World Alliance of Reformed Churches made a significant impact on many churches in South Africa. For a collection of articles exploring the topic see John W. de Gruchy and Charles Villa-Vicencio, eds., *Apartheid Is a Heresy* (Grand Rapids: Eerdmans, 1983).

10 For an argument as to why the term is misleading, see Ted A. Campbell, 'The "Wesleyan Quadrilateral": The Story of a Modern Methodist Myth', *Methodist History* 29 (1991).

11 Not too surprisingly, it remains unpublished, though one student was foolish enough to ask for a copy!

12 Stanley J. Grenz, *Revisioning Evangelical Theology: A Fresh Agenda for the Twenty First Century* (Downers Grove: Inter-Varsity Press, 1993).

13 As found in Stanley J. Grenz, *Theology for the Community of God* (Nashville: Broadman & Holman, 1994).

14 To utilize the categories of 1 Cor. 13:13.

15 He wanted to move beyond foundationalism, as it constructs its edifice on the basis of a foundation that is seen to be beyond dispute (for example, the trustworthiness of Scripture). Grenz felt this was inherently unstable, both because it reflects a modernist mindset in which one truth could be seen as foundational, but also because if the foundation was challenged, the entire system was likely to collapse. He therefore advocates webs of coherence, where overlapping sources help to strengthen the basis for beliefs.

16 Bebbington can be seen as representative when he suggests that biblicism is one of the defining characteristics of evangelicalism. Bebbington, *Evangelicalism in Modern Britain*, pp. 12–14.

17 Together with Franke, Grenz unpacks his understanding of this in Grenz and Franke, *Beyond Foundationalism*, pp. 57–92.

18 Ibid., pp. 60–63.

19 See e.g. Helseth's critique of Grenz's historical reconstruction in Paul Kjoss
    Helseth, 'Are Postconservative Evangelicals Fundamentalists? Postconserv-
    ative Evangelicalism, Old Princeton and the Rise of Neo-Fundamentalism',
    in *Reclaiming the Center: Confronting Evangelical Accommodation in Post-
    modern Times* (ed. Millard J. Erickson, Paul Kjoss Helseth, and Justin Taylor;
    Wheaton: Crossway, 2004).

20 Grenz, *Revisioning Evangelical Theology*, p. 87. The adequacy of this definition
    must be questioned. It implies a descriptive, rather than prescriptive, role for
    the theologian. Perhaps a church historian might be willing to be limited to a
    descriptive role, but it is improbable that many systematic theologians would be
    willing to accept such an abbreviated description of their task. Indeed, Grenz
    himself does not, for in spite of this definition, he carves out a far more ambi-
    tious role in his own theological work. Perhaps it should be enlarged to be a
    'reflection on the *adequacy* of the faith commitment of the believing community
    in the light of. . .' with relevant theological criteria inserted (e.g. Scripture, the
    tradition of the church, certain ethical criteria, etc.).

21 Ibid., p. 88.

22 Ibid., p. 93.

23 Ibid., p. 94.

24 The understanding of truth would be of truth as correspondent with objective
    reality.

25 Grenz, *Revisioning Evangelical Theology*, p. 112. While hard to dispute, this does
    seem to beg the question, Is it not the task of the theologian to articulate why
    this happens and how to evaluate the validity of such an 'encounter'? In addition,
    this presentation of the Pietists is one-sided according to Travis. See William G.
    Travis, 'Pietism and the History of American Evangelicalism', in *Reclaiming the
    Center: Confronting Evangelical Accommodation in Postmodern Times* (ed. Millard
    J. Erickson, Paul Kjoss Helseth and Justin Taylor; Wheaton: Crossway, 2004).

26 Brand accuses Grenz of driving an artificial wedge between those who focus on
    the Bible as a source of correct doctrine and those whose focus is on the Bible as a
    source of spiritual sustenance. Dismissing this typology as overly simplistic, Brand
    argues that balance between the two has usually characterized evangelicalism.
    Chad O. Brand, 'Defining Evangelicalism', in *Reclaiming the Center: Confronting
    Evangelical Accommodation in Postmodern Times* (ed. Millard J. Erickson, Paul
    Kjoss Helseth and Justin Taylor; Wheaton: Crossway, 2004), p. 298. Smith, in
    his work on the relationship between Pentecostalism and evangelicalism, is more
    nuanced when he distinguishes between evangelical theology and grass-roots
    evangelical experience. He writes, 'This issue [the relationship between Pente-
    costalism and evangelicalism] situates us in the midst of an ongoing historio-
    graphic debate between Donald Dayton and George Marsden . . . Dayton has

been insisting on a "pentecostal paradigm" for understanding evangelicalism over against what he calls Marsden's "presbyterian paradigm". I think both of them are right, but on different levels. I think Marsden is correct in asserting the dominant influence of the Princeton tradition on mainstream evangelical *theology*; but in agreement with Dayton, I think evangelicalism at a grass-roots level has been significantly influenced by a more Wesleyan-holiness piety as found, for instance, in Finney.' James K.A. Smith, 'The Closing of the Book: Pentecostals, Evangelicals, and the Sacred Writings', *Journal of Pentecostal Theology* 11, (1997): p. 61.

27 Grenz follows up on his own suggestion in *Theology for the Community of God*, and his discussion of Scripture in the middle of the book within the section on the work of the Spirit makes for a refreshing point of difference.

28 D.A. Carson, *The Gagging of God: Christianity Confronts Pluralism* (Grand Rapids: Zondervan, 1996), p. 481.

29 Grenz and Franke, *Beyond Foundationalism*, p. 94.

30 Which is not to suggest that the Reformers made no use of tradition. Attempts to literally apply *sola scriptura* are, inevitably, naive. While the Reformers held a theoretical commitment to *sola scriptura*, their hermeneutical practice is better described as *suprema scriptura*.

31 J. Wentzel Van Huyssteen, 'Tradition and the Task of Theology', *Theology Today* 55, no. 2 (1998): p. 217.

32 Grenz, *Revisioning Evangelical Theology*, pp. 95–7.

33 Both Carson and Erickson can be accused of responding superficially. D.A. Carson, 'Domesticating the Gospel: A Review of Grenz's Renewing the Center', in *Reclaiming the Center: Confronting Evangelical Accommodation in Postmodern Times* (ed. Millard J. Erickson, Paul Kjoss Helseth and Justin Taylor; Wheaton: Crossway, 2004); Millard J. Erickson, *The Evangelical Left: Encountering Post-conservative Evangelical Theology* (Grand Rapids: Baker, 1997); Millard J. Erickson, 'On Flying in Theological Fog', in *Reclaiming the Center* (ed. Millard J. Erickson, Paul Kjoss Helseth and Justin Taylor; Wheaton: Crossway, 2004).

34 Stanley J. Grenz, 'Culture and Spirit: The Role of Cultural Context in Theological Reflection', *Asbury Theological Journal* 55, no. 2 (2000): p. 40.

35 Donald G. Bloesch, 'Donald Bloesch Responds: On Grenz', in *Evangelical Theology in Transition: Theologians in Dialogue with Donald Bloesch* (ed. Elmer M. Colyer; Downers Grove: IVP, 1999), p. 186.

36 Grenz's comment that 'our theological reflection can draw from the so-called "secular" sciences, because ultimately no truth is in fact secular' and later that 'theology seeks to show how the postulate of God illumines all human knowledge' is important. Instead of the common evangelical reactionary default drive against that which is new in society, this approach allows the embracing of that which is not directly addressed in Scripture on the basis of the insights which

arise from the interaction. Stanley J. Grenz, 'What Does Hollywood Have to Do with Wheaton? The Place of (Pop) Culture in Theological Reflection', *Journal of the Evangelical Theological Society* 43, no. 2 (2000): pp. 310–311.

37 Grenz and Franke, *Beyond Foundationalism*, pp. 24–5.

38 Thomas C. Oden, *The Word of Life* (San Francisco: Harper & Row, 1992), pp. xv–xx.

39 While accepting the usefulness of seeking areas of consensus in the church's tradition, Harmon points out how fruitful times of dissent have been. Steven R. Harmon, 'The Authority of the Community (of All the Saints): Toward a Post-modern Baptist Hermeneutic of Tradition', *Review and Expositor* 100 (2003): pp. 611–612.

40 Macquarrie prefers to speak of formative factors as this clarifies that each factor is not on the same level or of the same importance. While acknowledging many formative factors, he discusses six: experience, revelation, Scripture, tradition, culture and reason. John Macquarrie, *Principles of Christian Theology* (London: SCM, rev. edn, 1977), pp. 4–18.

41 For example, Grenz very modestly suggests that 'the tradition of the Christian church serves as a source or a resource for theology, not as a final arbiter of theological issues or concerns but a hermeneutical context or trajectory for the Christian theological enterprise'. Even when speaking of the ecumenical consensus represented by statements such as the Apostles' and Nicene Creeds Grenz and Franke caution, 'Despite their great stature, such resources do not take the place of canonical scripture as the community's constitutive authority. Moreover, they must always and continually be tested by the norm of canonical scripture.' Grenz and Franke, *Beyond Foundationalism*, pp. 120, 124.

42 See Nicholas Wolterstorff, *Reason within the Bounds of Religion* (Grand Rapids: Eerdmans, 1976). The title of Wolterstorff's work is intentionally contra Kant. Immanuel Kant, *Religion within the Limits of Reason Alone* (trans. Theodore M. Greene and Hoyt H. Hudson; New York: Harper & Row, 1960).

43 Wolterstorff, *Reason with the Bounds of Religion*, p. 63.

44 Ibid., p. 64.

45 Ibid., p. 82.

46 For example: Which reading of Scripture? That which is appropriate for the embedded cultural context. But which cultural context? That which is consistent with Scripture . . .

47 Grenz's expression is 'the norming norm'. Grenz and Franke, *Beyond Foundationalism*, pp. 57–92.

48 He uses the expression in an article with the same title, which suggests that the truth of the gospel is ultimately that which frees and liberates. Stanley J.

Grenz, 'Participating in What Frees: The Concept of Truth in the Postmodern Context', *Review and Expositor* 100 (Fall 2003).

49 For a partisan account not limited to the role played by evangelicals but providing a useful overview of the way evangelicals understand their own contribution, see Schmidt, *Under the Influence*.

50 Jim Wallis laments, 'Evangelicals in [the twentieth century] century have a history of going along with the culture on the big issues and taking their stand on the smaller issues. That has been one of the serious problems of evangelical religion. Today, many evangelicals no longer just acquiesce to the culture on the larger economic and political issues, but actively promote the culture's worst values on these matters.' Wallis, *The Call to Conversion*, p. 25.

51 I am using 'bias' to help provide a range of descriptors. However, as bias has a pejorative tone, my inclination is to opt for the more positive 'privileging' or the more neutral 'preference'. However described, the goal is to attain methodological transparency.

11. A Closing Portrait: The Jesus Question

1 The Septuagint, also known as the LXX after the alleged seventy Jewish scholars who completed this translation in the late second century BCE.

2 See, for example, John 6:41–66; 8:13; 10:19ff.

The Tortoise Usually Wins

Biblical Reflections on Quiet Leadership for Reluctant Leaders

Brian Harris

The Tortoise Usually Wins is a theological exploration of the theory of quiet leadership aimed at those who reluctantly accept the mantle of leadership, but who often make a significant difference.

'Books on leadership are today two a penny. Just occasionally, however, one of these books might stand head and shoulders above most of the others, and to my delight *The Tortoise Usually Wins* falls into that category. I can see many church leaders benefitting from this book. I warmly commend this unusual book.'
Paul Beasley-Murray, Senior Minister, Central Baptist Church, Chelmsford; Chair of Ministry Today UK

978-184227-787-4

Leon Morris

*One Man's Fight for
Love and Truth*

Neil Bach

Leon Morris's story needs to be told. In this unique and long-awaited work Neil Bach shows Leon Morris as a prodigious and original thinker from the wrong side of the world who restored the credibility of evangelical scholarship and the centrality of the cross. Many of us have been nurtured by his enormously helpful books on the cross, but few know about the obstacles that had to be overcome. The author gives us a life of Leon Morris which is true to the man, unflinching in its evaluation of his work and inspiring in its conclusions. The book claims what evangelicals have widely acknowledged: Leon Morris was, and remains, Australia's most influential international scholar and pastor.

978-1-84227-986-1

The Big Picture

*Building Blocks of a
Christian World View*

Brian Harris

The Big Picture is an accessible and stimulating exploration of the big building blocks of the Christian faith. Harris's take on the big building blocks of Christian faith is refreshing and will be appreciated by all who would like to think through different ways to follow Jesus the Christ in an ever-changing context.

'Skilfully bringing together biblically-informed theology and the everyday world, Brian Harris unpacks themes of grace, creation and Christian hope in an engaging conversational manner. The result is a book that empowers us to live out our faith wherever we are.'
Stephen Garner, Laidlaw College, Auckland, New Zealand

978-1-84227-856-7

Paternoster is the theological imprint of Authentic Media, and publishes books across a wide range of disciplines including biblical studies, theology, mission, church leadership and pastoral issues.

You can sign up to the Paternoster newsletter to hear about new releases by scanning below:

Online:
authenticmedia.co.uk/paternoster

Follow us: